The Stately Ghosts of England

The Stately Ghosts
of
England

Diana Norman

DORSET PRESS

New York

First published in Great Britain 1963
by Frederick Muller Ltd.

This revised edition published 1977
by Robin Clark Ltd.

© Tom Corbett and Diana Norman, 1963, 1977

This edition published by Dorset Press,
a division of Barnes & Noble, Inc.,
by arrangement with Robin Clark Ltd.

1993 Dorset Press

ISBN 0-88029-208-3

Printed and bound in the United States of America

M 11 10 9 8 7 6 5 4 3

To my Grandparents

Acknowledgements

❀   ❀

MR. CORBETT and I would like to extend our most grateful thanks to all the ladies and gentlemen whose homes we visited, for their willing co-operation, unfailing kindness and unstinted hospitality.

I have reprinted the extract from *Edwardian Hey-Days* by George Cornwallis-West in my chapter on Salisbury Hall with the kind permission of the publishers, Putnam and Co. Ltd. The extract from *Morning Glory* by Mary Motley in the Brede chapter is reprinted with the permission of Longmans, Green and Co. Ltd.; and the extract from *My Crowded Sanctuary* by Clare Sheridan, in the same chapter, is reprinted with permission from Methuen and Co. Ltd. The two extracts from *Goodbye to All That* by Robert Graves are reprinted with kind permission of International Authors N.V. and Cassell and Co. Ltd.

My knowledge of Sir Francis Dashwood and the Friars of Medmenham comes largely from the book *Hell-Fire Francis*, by Ronald Fuller, published by Chatto and Windus.

My very warm thanks are due to Miss Helen Simpson and Mr. Jeremy Grayson for their excellent photographs, and I should like to take this opportunity to thank Tom Corbett for his unfailing patience with my ignorance of a subject in which he is a great specialist.   D.N.

Contents

✳   ✳

Illustrations

✳   ✳

Introduction

✻ ✻

SOME YEARS ago I was invited by Mr. Tom Corbett to
accompany him on his task of finding, clarifying and
cataloguing the ghosts that haunt some of England's
stately homes.

During the course of that weird and fascinating tour I
became converted from scepticism to a belief in ghosts;
that they haunt about eighty per cent of the historic houses
in Britain and that Tom Corbett has the gift of being able
to detect them.

Perhaps I should first explain to anyone who is as un-
acquainted with clairvoyants and their world exactly who
Tom Corbett is and what he does. It is almost easier to
say what he is not. He is *not* a medium. Mediums claim
that they are in touch with the spirit world through a
guide—a long-dead man or woman whose job it is to
bridge the gulf between the living and the dead. Clairvoyants make no such claim. They do not necessarily even
believe in spiritualism. Tom Corbett merely says that he
was born with the gift of getting glimpses into a world
that exists unseen and unfelt, except by a few, around and
in and beyond this one. As time in that world moves at a
different tempo, these glimpses include brief flashes of insight into the past, present and future.

Once, when I was interviewing Muriel Spark, the

novelist, she told me that she had what she described as an "invisible third ear", which was incessantly listening to what went on below the surface of the modern world. It made her aware of a supernatural force that was there behind the barrier, waiting to break through. It is an awareness that is constantly reflected in her writings.

Tom Corbett has not only this "third ear", but a third eye as well. He is very much a man of his time and yet, as he goes about, he is always aware of shadowy figures and sounds that are not available to most other people. It is not an exclusive gift. Most children have it and some of them manage to retain a little of it when they grow up—these are the people who see ghosts—but I know of no one who has developed it to such an acute degree as Tom, nor anyone who makes less fuss about it.

He has had six senses all his life and has learned to trust the sixth as he does the other five. He can tell if a house is haunted without knowing its history, pinpoint the scene of the haunting and, more often than not, say whether the ghost is a man or a woman.

He does not bother to lay traps for ghosts, try to trip them up with wire or take photographs of them with infra-red equipment because he dislikes wasting his time. You cannot, he says, prove ghosts to anyone who has never experienced them and does not want to believe in them. Ghosts cannot be put on the witness stand, or have their fingerprints taken. They are completely proof against proof.

His methods when ghost hunting are simply to walk through the house, picking up the vibrations and images that hauntings leave behind. He is the craftsman at work and when he gives his findings he has a craftsman's assurance in his own gift. The owners of the houses can take them or leave them. Most of them take them. His pronouncements were usually in exact accord with what they themselves had experienced. More often than not during our tour he pointed out, without prompting, the spot where they had seen the ghost and told them what form it took before they told him themselves.

My husband, one of the least gullible men I know, came with us on one of these visits and was as impressed by Tom at work as I had been.

I realise that all this will mean less than nothing to the sceptical reader. Well, that's all right. It is the sceptics' right to disbelieve, just as it is mine to print what I believe. I am not proselytizing on behalf of ghosts. You can lead a full, happy and useful life without believing in them. But I should like to point out that scepticism is largely a negative matter. People do not believe in ghosts because they have never come across them.

When I entered into the world of people who did give credence to the existence of ghosts, it was to find that it was populated by more intelligent, normal men and women than I, rather priggishly, had ever thought possible. There is a conspiracy in this country to regard a belief in the supernatural as the prerogative of sex-starved spinsters.

Within a matter of weeks of my conversion I picked up to re-read—quite by accident—two books by authors for whom I have a considerable respect. One was John Masters' account of his years among the Gurkhas, *Bugles and a Tiger*, the other was *Goodbye to All That*, Robert Graves' autobiography. Perhaps because I was now on the alert I found in both of them what I had missed before— an acceptance of ghosts.

John Masters mentions that the old army settlements of India were sometimes lit up by the long-extinguished flames that had been set alight by rebellious sepoys during the Mutiny. He says with complete authority that you can still hear the screams of the murdered women.

In *Goodbye to All That* Robert Graves mentions ghosts more than once as copper-bottomed fact. He wrote of one instance: "At Béthune, I saw the ghost of a man named Private Challoner, who had been at Lancaster with me, and again in 'F' Company at Wrexham. When he went out (to France in the First World War) to join the First Battalion, he shook my hand and said: 'I'll meet you again in France, sir.' In June he passed by our 'C' Company billet, where we were just having a special dinner to celebrate our safe return from Cuinchy—new potatoes, fish, green peas, asparagus, mutton chops, strawberries and cream, and three bottles of Pommard. Private Challoner looked in at the window, saluted, and passed on. I could not mistake him, or the cap-badge he wore; yet no Royal Welch battalion was billeted within miles of Béthune at the time. I jumped up, looked out of the window, and saw nothing except a fag-end smoking on the pavement. Challoner had been killed at Festubert in May."

To write a book about ghosts is rather like being a medical student—everybody tells you about their operation. Almost everyone I met had a real-life ghost story to tell me. And I began to find that Robert Graves' experience of having a friend come to say "good-bye" after that friend was dead, was not at all uncommon. During one of the inevitable conversations about ghosts, a girl friend of mine, a smart and intelligent secretary holding down a responsible job, said that the same thing had happened to her when she was much younger.

"I was at school at a convent," she said. "My favourite teacher was a nun called Sister Bridget. Then I got ill and had to spend some time in the convent infirmary. One day I looked up to see that Sister Bridget had come into my room. She smiled at me and I smiled back. Then she turned away and just walked through the wall. I began to scream at that, and the nuns came running to see what was the matter. I told them I had seen Sister Bridget and that she had disappeared. Then they told me that Sister Bridget had been taken ill and had died—a few minutes before I saw her."

For anyone who wants to go ghost hunting in England, there is a surprisingly wide choice of venue. Every year the national and local newspapers report dozens of incidents of ghost seeing. After studying these cuttings, I found that there was a certain pattern to them. About a quarter of the people reported having seen their ghost during visits to the historic homes, about another fourth of the incidents took place in aged pubs, and another, funnily enough, on council estates which, presumably, have been built on old sites.

It seems that the longer the history of a place, the greater is its chance of possessing a ghost. The other quarter of newspaper cuttings, incidentally, concerned miscellaneous ghosts who had been seen in a wide variety of blasted heaths, etc.

Assume that nine out of ten of these people are either mistaken, drunk or lying—though why they should be, beats me—and you are still left with a hard and considerable core of respectable men and women who have seen something supernatural.

In the stately homes, ghosts are a tradition, almost an inheritance, bequeathed from generation to generation. That is why Tom Corbett chose them to go ghost-hunting in. Over and above this, most of them have records that could substantiate his findings. Between us we chose a broad cross-section of these houses ranging from abbeys, great mansions and tiny, hidden manors, and found as big a variety of ghosts as we did residences.

The men and women who own these houses, whether they are titled or not, aristocrats or commoners, all live in a strange double world. They are part of the space age in which everything is scientifically rationalised, yet most of them have to accept that, in their own homes at least, they are in the midst of a definite, phantasmal activity.

They go out to work and carry on their business in a world that does not take the supernatural into account. But when they get home they are acutely aware that printless feet from the past are treading their corridors, that shadowy figures are lurking in dark corners, that invisible hands are opening and shutting the doors.

Ghosts are so much a part of their lives and inheritance that most of these house owners refer to them as commonplace fact, something that has to be taken into account and put up with. "We can't put Aunt Jenny in the arras room, the ghost would frighten her," was an attitude that I found to be the rule, rather than the exception, in the stately homes.

I am labouring this fact because, for me, it was this relationship between the ghosts and the people who have to live cheek by jowl with them that I found most fascinating of all. Also, I don't think it is sufficiently realised that many respectable, respected people in England are sharing their homes with ghosts, and know it, and have come to terms with it.

Gradually, however, the supernatural is becoming more "respectable" as far as the public is concerned. The presence of common-sense people like Tom Corbett is bringing back a greater trust in the much-maligned profession of clairvoyancy. Science has begun to express an interest. Even Oxford University has given its blessing to an investigation of extra-sensory perception.

Personally, I would welcome a re-awakening of scientific

interest in ghosts only because it might provide us with a better vocabulary for the supernatural and replace words like "manifestation", "visitation" and even "supernatural" itself, which have become overworked and out-moded but for which, at the moment, there are no substitutes. Apart from that I should be sorry to see science take over ghosts. I don't think it would ever satisfactorily explain them, and it would be a shame to see something so ethereal reduced to a mathematical equation.

Goodness knows, I do not contribute to derision of science. Still, there is a sneaking pleasure in knowing, as I know, that ghosts truly exist but that so far they have managed to slip through science's exploratory fingers.

*The Stately Ghosts
of England*

ONE

Longleat

❀   ❀

THE COLD in the passage had nothing to do with the April night outside. It was a dead, flat cold with sharply-defined boundaries, so that if you moved back a few paces you were out of it. My companions were shivering with it and even I, snug in my disbelief of what we were doing, was made uneasy.

Lord Christopher Thynne huddled himself a little deeper into his jacket and looked carefully at Tom Corbett.

"This is the passage," he said.

It looked a perfectly ordinary, newly-decorated corridor. It wasn't even on show to the public—just another passageway among the maze of passageways that thread through Longleat's top storey. But it had been distinguished from the others by the title "Green Lady's Walk" because, one by one, the generations of Thynnes at Longleat had become convinced that it was haunted by the spirit of their ancestress, Lady Louisa Carteret. And I was there that night because the head of the present generation, the Marquess of Bath, had decided to call in an expert, Tom Corbett, to try to prove it one way or the other.

Tom Corbett walked slowly up the passage, while we stood watching him and shivering. His hands were behind his back, and his head cocked a little to one side, like a farmer trying to gauge the weather.

"No," he said, slowly. "No."

He came back and led the way into another passage that was yawning on our right. As far as I could see it was indistinguishable from the first except that, if anything, the hideous cold was more intense.

From far out in the grounds came the hoot of an owl.

Tom turned to look at us. "There's something here," he said. "Something dreadful happened here. This is your corridor, not the other one."

There was a silence.

Miss Dorothy Coates who had been Longleat's librarian for a long time, looked at Lord Christopher. Then she spoke up. "You're quite right, Mr. Corbett. This is the 'Walk'. Christopher showed you the wrong corridor."

Tom was the only one of us who remained quite unmoved. He was used to being tested. He was also used to being right.

Lord Christopher and Miss Coates were more animated. They were pleased and excited in having proved their ghost-hunter and delighted that he had upheld what they had known for years—that the corridor was haunted.

But for Helen Simpson, who was with us to take photographs, and myself it was a revelation. We had to try to take in two revolutionary ideas.

We could not doubt, try as we might, that the incident we had just seen was genuine. Which meant that there really were people who had a psychic gift which, in turn meant, there was something for them to be psychic about.

The Fleet Street world in which we both moved did not recognise ghosts—or only as copy—and I had never even bothered to consider them. As far as I was concerned they existed only in the minds of the over-imaginative and that was that.

Now I had to shuffle all my ideas round to accommodate this revelation.

Probably there are people for whom that incident at Longleat would provide insufficient evidence on which to re-form the thinking of a lifetime.

I only know that standing there in that dreadful chill, high up in that deserted house with the owls hooting outside, watching a man pick out a haunted corridor from innumerable others . . . well, it was quite good enough for me.

. . . . .

A few days before, the features editor of the magazine I worked for had said, in that negligent way features editors have: "There's a clairvoyant going to go ghost-hunting at the Marquess of Bath's place. Fixed up for you and Helen Simpson to go down and cover it. It's an all-night job, but it should make a good piece."

Eleven years in journalism have conditioned me to being wrenched away from my husband and home to cover improbable stories. But I found the thought of this one more annoying than most.

Tom Corbett, when I met him to arrange details, however, was not the eccentric I dreaded. Instead, I found a silver-haired, sophisticated Irishman with the build of an ex-rugby player and a fair share of his national humour.

He immediately cleared the air. "I just happen to have been born with a psychic sense," he said. "It can happen to the nicest people. I didn't want it. I'd probably have been a happier man without it, but there it is.

"It works in two ways. For one thing, I can some-times tell people about themselves, occasionally seeing something about them in the future, sometimes in the past.

"For another, I can see ghosts. I haven't got any power over them, like exorcizing them or telling them to go away. But if there is a ghost around I can tell you where, and sometimes, what it looks like. Other people have this gift in varying degrees. Some, like me, see them, some hear them, others just sense them. Most people, of course, aren't psychic at all, so they won't ever see a ghost—even if it's standing right beside them.

"Ghosts, now—well, they are just people who have died and bound themselves, because of great happiness or great tragedy, to a spot on earth.

"When you are dead, you see, time doesn't exist. So a ghost can hang around for centuries by our reckoning, before it begins to fade away and get on to wherever it's going. That's all."

It was a lot, and Helen and I discussed it inconclusively as we drove down to Wiltshire, a day or two later, with Helen's inexhaustible supply of camera equipment loading down the back of the car.

We were to meet up with Tom at the mill-house on the outskirts of the Longleat estate where the Marquess of Bath and his family are living. It was in the beautiful drawing-room of the mill-house later that evening, that the Marquess told me the story of Longleat and, incidentally, laid the foundations for my coming conversion.

Like myself, Lord Bath is non-psychic. He never has seen and probably never will see a ghost. Normally this would be synonymous to saying that he does not believe in their existence, but it is not.

"I suppose, if I had been born into any other family," he said reflectively, "I would scoff at them."

But when Lord Bath became heir to Longleat and the

title, he also became heir to an entangling birthright of mystery, superstition, legend and hauntings bequeathed to him by twelve centuries' worth of English ancestors.

It is a legacy that is not easily shaken off.

Then again, he was conditioned. He was brought up in Longleat—which is generally acclaimed as one of the most ghost-ridden, atmosphere-laden houses in England. He managed to remain impervious to the ghosts, but not to their effect on other people.

And, finally, he saw built up in his lifetime a mosaic of small, strange events which, fitted together, gave a disquieting picture of a weird, grey world that exists alongside our own.

Like so many other ancient families, the Thynnes have hanging over their head a Damocles sword of superstition. They are doomed, it says, to die out if the swans, who have nested on the Longleat lakes for hundreds of years, should fly away and never return.

It is a superstition that is easier to laugh off if you are not actually living at Longleat, where it is devoutly believed by some of the older people in the surrounding villages, and where the swans are constantly circling just outside the windows.

Even so, it would be simpler to disregard, if it were not for something that happened in 1916.

Lord Bath's mother, the fifth Marchioness, was looking out of one of the windows when she saw five swans, flying low and making for the house. They circled round it, coming close to the window where she was standing. Suddenly one of the swans broke away from its companions and flew off into the distance, leaving the others to settle themselves on the lake.

All that day the young Lord Bath and his three sisters tried to dissuade their mother from her conviction that her eldest son, Viscount Weymouth, who was fighting with his unit in France, was dead.

The next day the telegram saying that he had been killed in action arrived. . . .

The fifth Marchioness had a strong psychic sense. She was aware of Longleat's ghosts and prey to its atmospheres. She was prescient more than once.

One morning, Lord Bath remembers, she came downstairs to join the family in the Great Hall. As she came into it, through the arch from the hallway, she seemed to brush aside an invisible curtain.

"Why are there men on the roof?" she asked. "And why are these dustsheets hanging here?"

There were no men, and no dustsheets.

But some time later a small fire broke out at Longleat, damaging the roof. Workmen were called in to mend it and, in order to stop the dust spreading, canvas was hung in the archways. . . .

Like so many other Elizabethan houses, Longleat is built on the foundations of a priory which disappeared at the Dissolution of the Monasteries. It seems that many monks who were turned out of their homes at that time vent a good deal of their spleen in cursing the future owners, or alternatively, anyone who tampered with the monastic burial grounds.

Longleat was not exempt.

However, a long succession of Thynnes—with one or two inevitable exceptions—have managed to live out quiet lives at Longleat. And, as no one knew where the burial grounds lay, the question of disturbing them did not arise. Then, one day, a gardener happened to dig up a skull. Before Lord Bath's father gave it burial in consecrated ground, five people handled that skull.

One of them was the young Lord Bath who, true to the

ghoulish tradition of small boys, put it on his head and rode round the grounds on his bike with it. Before the day was out, the four other people had all received some kind of injury and the Marquess had fallen from his bike and hurt himself badly. . . .

Undoubtedly the grimmest legend that Lord Bath grew up with was the one which said that his great-great-great-great-grandfather had murdered his wife's lover. It is a fact that it was quite a talking point of Queen Anne's day when Lady Louisa Carteret, daughter of the Earl of Granville, married the second Viscount Weymouth.

Even Sarah Jennings, the Duchess of Marlborough, remarked on the beauty and charm of Lady Louisa and found cause for amazement in her marriage. For Thomas Thynne, second Viscount, was, to judge from his portrait, a vacuous-looking, vicious-eyed man whose appearance, as far as we can see, was never belied by his actions.

According to the legend, the marriage turned out to be as miserable as gossip predicted. The inevitable happened—Lady Louisa met and fell in love with a young man whom she managed to smuggle into Longleat. They were discovered by her husband and a duel took place, fought up and down a corridor in Longleat's top floor. It ended in the death of the lover whose body—again according to legend—the Viscount buried beneath the cellar flagstones.

The corridor became known as Green Lady's Walk, because the portrait of the beautiful Louisa shows her dressed in green and because the legend went on to insist that her spirit walks up and down it in an agony of grief.

The facts fitted the legend, as far as they went. There is no doubt that the second Viscount moved away from Longleat about this time, as if he had conceived a horror for the place. He lived out the rest of his life at Horningsham, a nearby village, letting Longleat and its ground fall into disrepair.

Four generations of Thynnes, trying to forget this regrettable incident, came and went. Then, when the present Marquess was a young man, the legend took on a new and sinister probability. His father had decided to instal central heating at Longleat and set men to work laying the foundations for the system in the cellars. To do this they had to lift up the flagstones that paved the proposed boiler room.

It was there that they found the remains of what had once been a personable young man. He was dressed in clothing and boots that were identified as belonging to the time of Queen Anne. . . .

To add to all the old stories of the grey shape that had been seen walking along it, twentieth-century servants would go on ridiculously roundabout trips to avoid having to pass along it. Lord Christopher, the second of Lord Bath's three sons, conceived a horror for it and, even when he grew up, would make excuses to keep away from it after dark.

But the most telling evidence of all came from Longleat's highly-respected and efficient librarian, Miss Dorothy Coates. The effect of the corridor on her was such that at times she was quite unable to walk along it, and had to turn round and go back. She has described it as having an atmosphere of such misery and terror "that sometimes you daren't look behind you, you just dare not."

If the corridor had been the only haunted spot in the house the matter might have been left there. But it wasn't; there were other legends, other mysteries, other atmospheres.

The Marquess decided to call in an expert to try to find out exactly how many ghosts he owned.

Which is where we came in.

. . . . .

Longleat, a huge, Italian-style mansion, is impressive enough by day. By night it is awe-inspiring.

Its 11,000 acres surround it in silence. The swans that seem so strangely bound up with its fortunes look like alabaster figurines on the black, polished water.

The ghost-hunting expedition; Tom, Helen and myself with Lord Christopher and Miss Coates as guides had reached it about 11 p.m.

Tom's decision to carry out his investigations at night was based, he said, on the fact that ghosts are more apparent between midnight and 2 a.m.

If it was also slightly based on a sense of showmanship it was the last sign of this trait that we were to see that night. Tom's manner throughout was the unmoved, professional air of the man who has come to read the gas meter, rather than of a clairvoyant who had come to see about the ghosts.

But if he wasn't showing off, Longleat was. It had, without prompting, laid on all the atmosphere at its very considerable disposal. From the moment we entered by the cellars, it had enshrouded us in the quiet that belongs only to very old houses.

The brooding stillness of the grounds, and beyond them Salisbury Plain, was an ever present entity, pervading through the thick stone walls. The light, as we passed through the beautifully-proportioned rooms and hallways and mounted the stairs, had coaxed strange gleams from the eyes of the portraits that hung thick upon the walls.

Tom's voice cut through the silence that had come over all of us. "I think the murder took place here," he said, pausing at the end of the corridor where it leads into the Bishop Ken Library. "It is worst just here."

By now I was prepared to accept every word he said. The tension and the cold had become almost intolerable and brooked no disbelief. When we moved, hurriedly, into the Bishop Ken Library it was cut off as if someone had flicked a switch.

We had an appointment in the library—with Bishop Ken himself. When midnight came, it would be the anniversary of his death, over two centuries before. It was a long tradition in the family that he re-visited his old home on this night of the year although no one, as far as I could find out, had any grounds for this belief.

Bishop Ken was a high-principled and resolute churchman who first came to public notice while at Winchester. He was subjected to considerable pressure from the court to allow Nell Gwynne to lodge in the cathedral close—but refused.

Another king might have held a grudge against him, but Charles II could recognise an honest man when he saw one. Later, when the bishopric of Bath and Wells became vacant, he said: "Where is the good little man who refused his lodging to poor Nell?" and gave the appointment to Ken.

Under succeeding reigns, however, the Bishop's principles were regarded with less tolerance and he was deprived of his office. He sought, and found, sanctuary with his great friend the first Viscount Weymouth, who gave him a home at Longleat for the next twenty years of his life, spending most of his time in the Old Library that now bears his name.

Tom was doubtful about Bishop Ken's haunting. Ghosts in his experience, he said, didn't turn up on the dot at set times in fact, only in fiction. He spent most of the time until midnight patiently answering my basic questions on ghost-lore, as I tried hard to orientate myself into this new world. Having been an avid horror-story reader in my youth, I found it difficult to rid myself of the fictionalised image of ghosts.

Why, I wanted to know, did Louisa Carteret haunt the passage and not the more logical shades of her husband and lover? And how did he know it was Louisa anyway and not the husband and/or lover?

Tom smiled. "I don't know it is Louisa," he said, "I'm just assuming it is. The ghost is certainly a woman. A spirit retains the identity and sex it had when it was alive.

"The men don't haunt, presumably, because they had what it takes to progress, while Louisa's grief kept her shackled here."

The very name that had been given to the place, "Green Lady's Walk", denoted, he said, that the various people who had experienced the ghost in the passage had known without question, that it was the spirit of a woman they had encountered.

He doubted, however, if they had ever actually seen her in green, and thought that this embellishment was merely prompted by the picture of her in her green dress.

"In my experience, ghosts rarely manifest themselves in colour," he said. "They're usually seen and described as grey or whitish-grey—because this is the general colour of the ectoplasm which surrounds psychic manifestations."

Later, checking cuttings on "Ghosts" in the newspaper library, I found that Tom was right. The vast majority of the hundreds of ghosts who have been reported by the general public over the last ten years have been described as grey.

We fell quiet as midnight came and went. Then Tom, who had been studying a sixteenth-century French bible, lifted his head.

"I'm sorry," he said apologetically. "I can't get anything. I don't think Bishop Ken haunts the house."

That obviated one ghost at least, but there were others to come.

We moved on—this time downstairs to the Red Library. It is one of the anomalies of Longleat that, although all the rooms are served by the same central-heating system, they all have markedly different temperatures.

By the time we reached the Red Library we seemed to have passed through degrees ranging from humidity to ice. The Library, however, retained something of the welcoming warmth it had when it was the family's favourite sitting-room, although it is now on show to the public.

Associating, as I did, ghosts with the chill we had felt upstairs, it was rather surprising to hear Miss Coates say that the long, book-lined room was haunted.

"But it's a completely different ghost from the one in the corridor," she said. "It's companionable, friendly. I've worked in here a lot and all the time I've been conscious that there was somebody standing, just out of view, watching me. I think of him as the 'nice, kind gentleman'. I know it's a man, and I know it's friendly.

"Every time I look round, of course, he isn't there. But the impression from the corner of my eye that he is standing there is very strong. Once when I was working I thought he said something. It seemed so natural that I opened my mouth to say, 'I'm sorry, I didn't hear what you said'—and then I realised how ridiculous it was."

When Miss Coates had mentioned her ghost to the family, somebody had remembered an incident which took place when Lady Caroline, the Marquess' elder daughter, was a little girl.

It seems she had been in the Red Library with her

nanny when she asked, "Who's that old gentleman who's just gone through the door?"

The nanny was up and into the next room with speed. There was no one there. But nothing could shake Lady Caroline's conviction that she had seen an "old gentleman".

As Miss Coates finished speaking, Tom crossed the room to stand by the bookcase on the right of the fireplace.

"He stands here, doesn't he?"

Miss Coates nodded, impressed.

"Fairly tall. In a long black robe. Age about fifty, even sixty. That right?"

"It's certainly the impression I've got of him."

Tom nodded. "I can't be sure," he said, "but I have the feeling he built this place."

In that case Miss Coates' ghost was none other than Sir John Thynne, that wealthy Elizabethan gentleman. And if anyone loved their home enough to come back to it after death, he did.

The original priory, which he bought in 1540, for £53, was burnt down. Immediately he started to build a new home, one worthy of his status and wealth. He spent an immense amount of time superintending every detail of the building. After a year, however, all his work was destroyed—again by fire.

Patiently, and with the same eye for detail, Sir John started all over again, lavishing money and care on it until it was completed, twelve years later.

When he finished he had a 100-room mansion, a perfect example of the Italian style, which at least three monarchs of England—including the ubiquitous Elizabeth I—have stayed at and been graciously pleased to admire.

And now, four hundred years later, his spirit had to

stand and watch as a small party of people ambled about his empty home looking for ghosts.

This time we were on our way to, of all places, the linen cupboard in the servants' quarters.

Once more this was at the instigation of Miss Coates who wanted Tom to have a look at it.

Like the corridor, it is a place she fears. "I can't say why. It has a horrible feeling about it. I'd like to know what Mr. Corbett thinks of it."

But it was while on our way to the servants' wing that probably the strangest happening of that strange night took place.

We had reached that section of the house in which Miss Coates used to sleep before she moved to her present house in the Stables Courtyard. When we reached her old bedroom and were admiring it, Tom—who was in the doorway—suddenly lifted his hand and knocked, once, on the door.

For a second Miss Coates froze and then she asked, "Why did you do that?"

Tom shrugged his shoulders. Like everything else that night, the action had been dictated by his sixth sense.

"Well, it's a very funny thing," said Miss Coates, "but during the time I slept in this room there was never a night when something didn't knock on that door. Always about the same time. Only one knock. Of course, when I opened the door there was no one there, so I stopped opening it. It really was most alarming because it couldn't have been anyone in the house."

And that was that. Just another small, unexplained incident that anyone who goes ghost hunting has to take in his stride. Ghosts are never neat and logical. Sometimes we are lucky enough to have a legend or piece of history handed down which explains their actions. Mostly they go on haunting—seemingly aimlessly—long after the reasons for their haunting have been forgotten by anyone alive.

And so, in the shadows of an empty house, this sad thing continues to knock at a door . . . and nobody will ever know why.

·   ·   ·   ·   ·

The next day, after breakfast, Tom delivered his report to Lord and Lady Bath, as one who recounts a bag of grouse.

"Certainly two very strong ghosts," I heard him say. "The one in the corridor and the one in the Red Library. Then there's another, very faint, which causes the knock on Miss Coates' door. There's a heavy malevolence in the linen cupboard caused, I think, by someone who was probably once a housekeeper—a most unpleasant woman.

"All the hauntings are done independently, and each ghost is unaware of the others' existence. But our intrusion wasn't welcome, I'm afraid. The Bishop Ken doesn't haunt, by the way."

And I heard the Marquess say, "Glad of that. I never could see why he should."

Driving back through the deserted parkland in the early hours I had wondered if my new-found belief in ghosts would survive the morning.

To my surprise it had.

The sanity of the sun, and the reassuring sound of clinking breakfast cups had not detracted from the drama of the night—only thrown it into relief. For better or worse, it seemed, I was now a believer in ghosts.

But it was comforting to know, as I looked around at Lord and Lady Bath listening intently to what Tom told them, that at least I was in good company. It was less comfort, however, to find a fortnight later when I had recovered from a slight bout of pleurisy that both Tom and Helen had been ill.

"I *knew* we weren't welcome," said Tom, darkly.

.　　　.　　　.　　　.　　　.

A month or so later Tom rang me. He had, he said, been so intrigued by his findings at Longleat that he intended to go on similar expeditions to other stately homes. Would I, he asked, like to go along, too, as Boswell to his Johnson.

I had been equally intrigued. I said I would.

TWO

Littlecote

❋   ❋

IN HIS BOOK, *Exploring English Character*, Mr. Geoffrey Gorer analysed the answers to 5,000 questionnaires sent to a cross-section of the public.

He estimated from these that one-sixth of England's population believes in ghosts and that a further quarter keeps an open mind on the subject.

I believe, however, that if a survey was carried out among the owners of the houses that are ghost-prone, i.e. the historic and ancient homes, the proportion of believers would balance, if not outweigh, the sceptics and don't-knowers.

It seems to me significant that out of thirty letters sent out at random to stately home owners last year, I received only two sceptical replies.

The letters asked the owners if they had any ghosts and, if so, whether they would allow us to investigate them.

I was very sensitive about them. The request "Have you any ghosts?" would, I felt, seem the proverbial silly question that deserves a silly answer.

But, as I say, I only had two "silly answers".

One was from a well-known baron who protested indignantly and a little too much that his was a "happy" home. The funny thing was that my letter to this baron had been prompted by information given by one of his own former employees who had approached Tom suggesting the investigation. "I have never known such a haunted house," the man had said. "At night, when everyone is in bed, the place is terrorised by voices and peals of music."

The other was a letter of amused disbelief from the distinguished baronet, the late Sir John Dashwood, whose home in the eighteenth century was the headquarters of the infamous "Hellfire Club" and its equally infamous founder Sir Francis Dashwood.

In my sensitivity I chose to regard the letter as sarcastic, and replied in kind. Sir John and I then entered into a lengthy and acrimonious correspondence which delighted us both and led to his invitation to visit the Hellfire caves—with results which I shall deal with later.

The other twenty-eight replies were prompt, courteous and sympathetic, showing an acceptance of ghosts as widespread as it was surprising. Among those who have inherited their homes from a long progression of ancestors, this acceptance was almost automatic—a just as integral, if less publicised, part of their upbringing as the old school tie.

What was less expected, though, was the almost enthusiastic response from the newer gentry who have moved into the stately homes in the last fifty years or so.

It seems that you cannot breathe in daily the atmosphere of ancient feuds, romances, births and deaths without coming round to the view that there *are* more things in heaven and earth. . . .

The Wills family, for instance, have owned Littlecote, just over the Wiltshire border from Hungerford, for only fifty-five years.

Sir Ernest Wills, the tobacco magnate and the grandfather of the present owner Mr. D.S. Wills, bought Littlecote

38

in 1922. In 1958 his son, Major Wills, inherited its 6,000 acres and two years later opened it to the public. But the fifty-five years have been enough for Littlecote to work its spell and make the Willses recognise the existence of its ghosts. And Major Wills' letter said that he would be pleased to meet us at Littlecote and show us over it personally.

.   .   .   .   .

I was sitting on a beautifully-carved stone bench near the front door of Littlecote.

Behind me was the mellow Tudor façade of the house, and a deep blue border of lavender in which the bees were working very hard.

In front of me was the deep, wide lawn which ended in the old brick wall that surrounds the garden. Beyond that again swept up a hill that was blending with a shimmering sky.

It was very hot.

We had been given, like other visitors, our tour of the house and were now waiting for Major Wills to take us on our private view.

Tom was off somewhere at the back of the house, talking to the man at the trout hatcheries. Helen had gone off on her single-minded quest for pictures.

Even the visitors weren't in sight. They were inside walking through the cold corridors and gaping, as we had, at some of the most beautiful rooms in England, at the inevitable Elizabeth the First bedroom, at the chapel where Cromwell's troops worshipped, and at the Great Hall where Charles II forgave Littlecote and its head for their defection during the Civil War as he ate a "costly" dinner.

I was alone, trying to fight off the soporific effect of the

39

sun and imagine the state of mind of a woman who lived 400 years ago. And a tough old woman she must have been. She was known as Mother Barnes, and she lived at Great Shefford, three or four miles away from Littlecote, where she was the local midwife.

My knowledge of Elizabethan midwives is scanty, and discouraging. If Ma Barnes lived to the rule she was bawdy and ignorant. Her methods of dealing with childbirth were crude and unhygienic. She probably lost as many mothers as she saved.

But none of this warranted what happened to her on that dark, wild night in 1575.

For it was then that two men rode out of the rain up to her door and demanded that she go with them. They said they had come to take her to a lady who was in labour, that they would pay her well, but that she must submit to being blindfolded so that she wouldn't be able to identify the house.

It must have sounded fishy, even to her, but she went. And a dreadful ride it was, bumping pillion behind one of the servants through the storm with a bandage over her eyes.

She kept her head, though, and when, towards dawn, they arrived at their destination, she still had enough sense to count the number of steps she had to climb and the number of chambers she passed through.

Later this was to help her identify the house.

Then someone must have taken off her bandage. For there before her stood a "tall slender gentleman having upon hym a longe goune of blacke velvett".

Frightened though she already was, Ma Barnes would have been terrified had she known who the gentleman was. For Ma Barnes had been brought to Littlecote and the man before her was the owner, Will Darrell who, even in those tempestuous days, had earned for himself the nickname "Wild".

At Longleat they have a satire which Will Darrell wrote to his contemporary, Sir John Thynne, when he was building Longleat, jeering at Longleat's Italian style. But Sir John had the last laugh. He was founding a home for his descendants, but Darrell had come to the end of his line. Evil-liver and spendthrift that he was, he was the last Darrell to own Littlecote.

He hissed at Mother Barnes that she was to attend to a lady in the next chamber, and "yf shee be safely delivered, yow shall not fayle of great rewards, but if shee myscarry in her traveyle, yow shall dye." Whereupon, "as one amased", poor old Mrs. Barnes went into the richly hung bedroom and the labouring woman who lay behind the drapes of the bed.

As if the night wasn't dreadful enough, a further macabre touch had been added, for the woman was masked.

Some time later Mrs. Barnes came wearily out of the bedroom with a baby boy in her arms. Back in the room lay a dying woman. But, after all, this wasn't an out-of-the-way occurrence, and she had at least managed to save the child. I should imagine she felt fairly proud of herself.

But once more in front of her was the awful man in black velvet and, madly, he was telling her to throw the baby on the fire.

Mrs. Barnes protested and begged on her old knees for the child's life, promising that she would bring it up herself, look after it as her own. But the child was thrown on the fire and a half-crazed woman was escorted back to Shefford, back to the stolid existence she had led before. I doubt, however, if things were ever the same for her again.

The amazing thing was that she kept her mouth shut

for fourteen years. Then, afraid that she might die with it on her conscience, she went to a magistrate and made a deposition.

It is only from this—which I have quoted—and some contemporary letters that we know as much as we do, because Darrell was never brought to trial. He lived on to go into a debtors' prison and be released. But in 1589 he went hunting in Littlecote park, was thrown by his horse and broke his neck.

"The place where he was killed is still called 'Darrell's Stile'," Mrs. Wills told me later. "And to this day horses will shy frantically if they are ridden past it."

Major Wills, although he doesn't bruit it about, believes that the woman in the mask may have been Will Darrell's sister. There seems to be little other explanation for the murder of a child by a man who undoubtedly had more than his fair share of illegitimate progeny.

There is, of course, a ghost attached to all this, otherwise we wouldn't have been down at Littlecote on that hot, July afternoon.

Legend has it that the mother of the murdered child haunts Littlecote—as well she might. But what had tempted us down was the fact that a ghost of a woman had been seen by one of the Willses themselves—Sir Edward de Winton Wills, Major Wills' elder brother.

I have said that I have never seen a ghost, and I haven't. But I think I got close to it that afternoon at Littlecote as I waited for the visitors to leave. If the darkness and cruelty of Will Darrell showed the worst side of Elizabethan life, the scene before me was redolent of the best—the sun, the graceful lawn, the warm brick. It had a suspended air as if it were waiting for a woman with ruff and farthingale to walk on and complete it. The slight breeze had died away, so that the sound of the bees grew louder, and it seemed to me that if I sat there long enough something would happen. All that did happen, though, was the emergence of the visitors from the house, and the spell was broken.

But that wasn't the end of it, because later I spoke to one of the guides who shows the tourists round Littlecote and it was her contention that the garden was haunted.

"Only a few weeks ago," she said, "I saw a woman standing by the herbaceous border waiting, as I thought, to come in. Immediately I went out to fetch her. I must have arrived there seconds after I'd seen her but she wasn't there, or anywhere in sight. I searched for her but she had disappeared—she can't have had time to walk off. I think what I saw was a ghost."

And even *that* wasn't the end of it.

For, as we all moved into the house to meet Major and Mrs. Wills, Tom, who had been wandering around, said pleasantly as he shook hands: "I see you have a ghost in your garden"—rather as most people would remark on the beautiful flowers.

Major Wills took it very well. "Oh yes?" he said, politely.

"A woman," said Tom, "rather beautiful. I got the impression that she was barred from the house in some way. Oh, and I got the feeling of draped horses moving across the lawn."

That time he struck oil. Littlecote, Major Wills told us, lies directly across the site of what had once been a well-used Roman road.

Major Wills himself has never seen a ghost. He is prejudiced in their favour, however, partly because of his brother's experience and partly because of the atmosphere that pervades Littlecote.

"When I was much younger," he said, "there were rooms that had a definite sinister feeling about them. I've noticed, though, that their atmosphere changed slowly. We were a happy family and since we've lived here the feeling of the house has become mellower, kinder. I think our influence has got rid of whatever was turbulent in the house."

And, indeed, walking in and out of the shafts of golden light that came through the Littlecote mullion windows was in sharp contrast to our progress through Longleat.

Littlecote was built somewhere between 1490 and 1520 in place of an earlier house dating from the thirteenth century. After Wild Will broke his neck it became the property of Sir John Popham, Lord Chief Justice under Elizabeth—his fat, gross-looking portrait hangs in the hall. The Pophams held it until 1922 when Sir Ernest Wills bought it.

We went into the Great Hall first. It was high and beautiful and the yellow jerkins and round helmets of the Cromwellian troops who were garrisoned at Littlecote during the Civil War hung emptily on the walls. From there we went into the quiet comfort of the library, drenched with a Gainsborough evening sun and on into the cool Brick Hall with its brick floor and black oak panelling. It wasn't until we got into the robing room next to the chapel that we struck anything.

Immediately, Tom said: "There's a clear image here of a little man, a nice old chap, happy and quiet. He is short and thickset, probably a priest and almost definitely a recluse—he used this room a lot."

He led the way on into the pride and joy of Littlecote— the Cromwellian chapel. It is the oldest part of the house and the finest example of a Cromwellian conversion in England.

Its tall black pews where the Roundheads once wor- shipped under the whitewashed walls and plain gallery are very lovely. The plain black cross fixed high on the wall over the pulpit looks more impressive than the most ornate crucifix.

I began to worry in case Tom's ecstatic preoccupation with the glass candle bowls in the gallery would interrupt his concentration. After all, we were now nearing the Haunted Landing where Will Darrell became an infanticide and where the tormented mother is supposed to walk.

We reached it as the sun went over the hill where Darrell lost his life, and we stood in its last light watching Tom as he walked to the huge fireplace and rested his hand on the mantel.

There was no chill, no malevolence, nothing to indicate an unhappy ghost, as there had been in Longleat's haunted corridor.

After a long time Tom said: "I'm sorry. There just isn't anything here. Are you sure this is the right place?"

"Try the bedroom where the child was born," suggested Mrs. Wills.

In the Littlecote brochure this particular room is called "The Haunted Bedroom"—but Tom came out as puzzled as he went in.

"There's nothing there. Are you sure the child was born there, or have you changed the room around much? There's something that doesn't fit—doesn't belong."

I don't think Tom could have said anything that would have delighted the Willses more. It is only tradition that says the landing and bedroom are *the* landing and *the* bedroom. And the epithet "Haunted" has been given to them purely as a courtesy title. Nobody has ever found the atmosphere there appalling. The most psychic of guests have slept sweetly in the "haunted" bedroom. Yet the tradition of a haunting there has persisted sufficiently to become famous.

That Tom refused to substantiate a ghost there proved his worth to Major and Mrs. Wills better than if he had come up with a dozen hand-wringing phantoms.

"What is more," Major Wills told us, "the room is not as it was in Darrell's day. The original bed went to America, and those are most certainly not the original drapes."

On our way to the *really* haunted part of the house, we made a detour at the request of Mrs. Wills to visit a bedroom in which she had slept, and which she considered disturbed.

To get there we had to climb a flight of stairs overshadowed by a stained glass window.

Halfway up Tom paused and sniffed. We all sniffed.

"A whiff of incense," said Tom. He was right . . . the slightest ephemeral smell . . . but quite definitely incense.

Major Wills said "It's always here," as if to have an unexplained waft of incense floating about the house were the most normal thing in the world. But it was a phenomenon we were to encounter quite frequently in other houses we visited, in most of which incense had not been used for four hundred years.

The bedroom—it is known as the Chinese bedroom—interested Tom immediately.

He walked around it for a moment or two and then summed it up as being haunted by a "busybody". It was a curious sort of word to describe a ghost, but it delighted Mrs. Wills.

"That's it exactly," she said. "I have woken up in the night in this room with the conviction that someone was bustling about—a busybody, as you say."

In an atmosphere of mutual approval we moved off to the scene of Sir Edward's encounter with the ghost. It proved to be the Long Gallery, a room connecting one part of the house to the other, and a hundred and ten feet long.

We entered it by an inconspicuous door at one end. Right away Tom said, "It wasn't up here your brother saw the ghost—it was the other end."

Of course, he was right, and we began to walk down. But when we were half way along there was an interruption. Out of the blue Tom demanded to know who had lived in the house that had limped.

Major Wills searched his memory hard and could only think of a Mr. Bevan who had rented the house just after the First World War. "He was later mixed up in a swindle of some sort. I think he limped," he said.

"Well, he's still here," said Tom.

Gerard Lee Bevan, if I may digress for a bit, caused as big a scandal in the 1920s as any of Wild Will Darrell's rip roaring exploits in the days of the first Elizabeth.

During his tenancy of Littlecote he was admired as a man of substance and respectability. Educated at Eton and Oxford he was highly religious, a non-smoker and total abstainer. He came of a family of astute bankers and financiers and was so highly thought of that during the 1914-18 War the Government made him Tobacco Controller.

But at the age of fifty something must have snapped in his respectable brain. He began to drink. He took up with women and he took up with crime. As the completely trusted director of dozens of companies and chairman of the City Equitable Fire Insurance Company, he was able to swindle on a grand scale.

On February 8, 1922, he and a woman friend boarded a plane for Paris—the first time in criminal history that someone had absconded by plane. Behind him the City Equitable shares slumped to bottom and the liabilities of companies involved in the crash were estimated at four million pounds.

A huge hunt was laid on to find him. The *Daily Mail* offered £500 reward for information leading to his arrest. But Bevan was racketing about the Continent so fast that no one could catch up with him. He grew a beard and posed as an artist.

Eventually he was betrayed by a woman and arrested at Innsbruck and brought back to England, where he was given a seven-year sentence. He was released from jail in 1928, went abroad and died in Havana aged sixty-six.

It is an improving thought, if true, that his ghost has come back to the calm and respectability it once knew at Littlecote.

At the other end of the Gallery, Major Wills told us the story of his brother's ghost: In the year 1927 Sir Edward brought his wife to stay at Littlecote. They were given a bedroom leading off from the Long Gallery. Every night of their stay they were woken up in the early hours by the frantic barking of their pekingese dog, Sunny, who slept in their room. The barking lasted only a minute or two and then Sunny would settle down again.

Sir Edward was intrigued by the behaviour of the peke and one night, when he woke to find Sunny going nearly mad and pointing like a gun dog towards the door, he got up and went out into the passageway. He was just in time to see the figure of a woman with an old-fashioned rushlight in her hand walking away from him and then disappear.

Unruffled, Sir Edward made a search which satisfied him that what he had seen was not a human intruder and he went back to bed. The following day the whole household was told about the visitation and an old head housemaid came forward with additional information.

It was her job to do the rounds last thing at night and

The haunted Long Gallery at Littlecote

The courtyard at Penfound Manor

Salisbury Hall in Winter

see that Littlecote's many windows were firmly shut. "And often when I come to this part of the house," she said, "I would see a lady wandering around wearing a sort of pink dressing gown."

"She seemed quite happy about it," said Major Wills. "She didn't want to leave or anything, so the ghost can't have been very frightening."

But, as Major Wills had said, the atmosphere at Littlecote has changed a great deal since then—the turbulent has subsided into comparative content.

Try as he might, Tom could find no evidence that the Long Gallery is now haunted at that end, although he is convinced that it was in that part of the house that the Darrell incident took place, and not in the so-called "Haunted Landing".

"There's still a slight feeling there," he said. "But it's so faint that it's only a kind of memory. Ghosts have to fade away sometime or other. They can remain tied to one spot for centuries but eventually they realise that they must progress."

Slowly we meandered through the rest of the beautiful house. Once Tom remarked, "Your mother was a very strong character wasn't she?"

"Very," said the Major. "The whole house is still full of her."

Apart from that Tom kept very quiet. It seemed to me that he was looking for something, and was studying hard the portraits that abounded on the walls. But it wasn't until we came to the Regency Room that he found what he wanted.

"There's the woman," he said, excitedly for him. "That's the woman who's haunting your garden. I was hoping to see her picture somewhere in the house."

The painting showed a lovely and assured woman

dressed in the elegant, high-waisted dress of the Regency period. The caption read: "Mrs. Leybourne Popham".

"Why is she in the garden?" asked Tom, "and why wasn't she allowed in the house?"

But the Willses were unable to help. "I can't think," said Mrs. Wills. "We don't know much about her, I'm afraid. If there had been a scandal, her portrait wouldn't have been allowed to hang here, surely. Unless, of course, she had contracted some illness which had forced her to keep away from her family."

In the painting itself Mrs. Popham is shown in the garden, and not indoors like the subjects of most of the other portraits at Littlecote. But why such a woman should haunt the garden—and presumably she is the ghost that the guide saw—we shall never know.

Tom had, however, demonstrated enough of the accuracy of his gift of second sight to make Major and Mrs. Wills believe him and assured that, if only sufficient investigation could be carried out on the life of Mrs. Popham, it would show that for some reason she had been barred from entry into the house.

And that was more or less that. It was an anti-climactic and inconclusive end to the hunt for one of the most famous and publicised ghosts in England. Instead, Tom had found three minor ghosts whose only common denominator was that none of them haunted the haunted landing. But this is a factual account and I can't help it if real ghosts are less imaginative and tidy than the fictionalised versions of them. We were to find drama enough later on.

Anyway, the Littlecote chapter is only satisfactory or unsatisfactory according to your point of view. For me it was pleasant to think, as we walked away from Littlecote across the emerald lawn, that its ghosts are fading away from it as gently as the sun was then fading over Darrell's hill.

THREE

Woburn Abbey

IT WOULD BE WRONG to give the impression that the stately homes flaunt their ghosts.

An attempt to present the ghosts of famous houses as a tourist attraction was made by the British Travel and Holidays Association some time ago. But it was not really successful.

For one thing, ghosts do not make good publicity gimmicks. They are too indecisive, too ephemeral. For another there was a squeamishness on the part of the owners of stately homes to bare their hauntings to the public. They were willing, in a few cases, to include the legend of a ghost in their brochures and guides, but proved reticent about giving their own experiences of it.

This reticence arose from two inhibitions: One, the difficulty of putting across the atmosphere, influences and sensations of a haunting to a sceptical public. Two, the traditional belief that it is not nice to discuss personal matters and feelings. And your own ghosts *are* a personal matter, usually deeply felt.

Tom Corbett's success in getting people to talk about their reactions to haunting as much as they have is due to the fact that they know he is on their side, believing implicitly in ghosts, and understanding what it is to experience them. To him they unburden themselves, rather as a patient will list every ache and pain to an understanding doctor. To the public, however, they have kept up a consolidated, indifferent front.

Even where there has been the personal experience of a ghost the brochure will only mention that a certain room "is supposed to be haunted".

This was the case at Longleat and Littlecote. And the guide book of Beaulieu (see Chapter Eleven) makes no reference to hauntings at all—although it is probably cne of the most ghost-ridden homes in the country.

The most surprising omission of all, however, is contained, or rather not contained, in the brochure of Woburn Abbey.

Now if ever a house and its master have bared their soul to the world it is Woburn and the Duke of Bedford. By a constant stream of clever publicity promotions and gimmicks, the Duke of Bedford has achieved his aim and made Woburn the most popular stately home in the business. Nothing that would make Woburn more congenial, attractive and intriguing to the public has been left out or undone—yet the mention of hauntings is conspicuously absent.

One might think that this is because there is nothing to reveal—that the tramp of 30,000 visitors a week during the season have stamped out what ghosts there were.

One would be wrong.

Behind the façade of tea rooms, roundabout, souvenir shops and coach rides, lie five hundred years of very considerable history. And the psychic burden of those years lies heavy over the house. It was to affect and trouble Tom Corbett more than any other house we visited.

The Duke of Bedford himself is extremely susceptible to his ghosts. Modern and brilliantly publicity-prone though he is, he inescapably remains the son of his forefathers. His ancestors are very real to him. In their greatness they made Woburn into something that he loves and needs. Then, in their weakness, they left him with no say in the running of his own estate, which is in the hands of trustees.

When at the age of thirty-six, he found himself the thirteenth Duke of Bedford, he also found himself committed to paying off four and a half million pounds in death duties—or losing Woburn. Despite the tremendous difficulties he knew it would entail, he chose Woburn.

Add to this awareness of past and duty a highly-developed psychic sense and you will realise that the Duke of Bedford is a very haunted man. Probably his ghosts are the only part of his inheritance he has not had to exploit in his chosen task of keeping Woburn constantly before the public eye. They remain, literally, behind locked doors in the private part of the house (now occupied by the Marquess of Tavistock and his family), and the public, as it wanders around the rest, knows nothing about them.

· · · · ·

On the day that we visited him at Woburn, the Duke's diary read: "Morning: Give B.B.C. talk on dairy farming. Afternoon: Receive Japanese Ambassador. Evening: Tea with ghost hunters."

He took us all in his stride. Tom and I found, for instance, that there was no question of working the Duke round to our point of view on ghosts. He was already there, waiting for us to catch up.

His first introduction to psychic matters, he told us, came when he was a very young man, doing the social round.

"I went to a house party given by Lord Tredegar at his place down in Wales. He was a very odd man, extremely interested in the supernatural, and one night when we were all sitting in his room in front of a huge fire he put on some old cabbalistic clothing and told our fortunes.

"There was an owl flying round the room, and it was all very eerie. But the funny thing was that while he was telling these fortunes, the temperature of the room dropped like a stone. Although I was right in front of that fire, I was freezing."

It is an experience with which I personally can sympathise. The same thing once happened to me, at an exorcism ceremony I covered years ago for my newspaper. It was a little house in South London on a cold day. The fire was roaring up the chimney, the small room was crammed with exorcists, commentators and reporters. Arc lights flooded the scene, which was being televised. It was stifling.

For some reason I was invited to sit in the circle. The medium and arch exorcist, an underground train driver in normal life, if I remember correctly, went into a trance. And by the time he came out of it my hands were blue with cold. Somehow I squared this incident with my disbelief in the supernatural—until Longleat.

The Duke also forgot about the Tredegar incident—until Woburn.

He was first introduced to the Abbey when he was sixteen, not having known before that he was heir to the estate or the dukedom—or even that they existed. In fact, he first learned he was heir to a Dukedom from a gossiping maidservant.

For this ignorance he had to thank his father, an eccentric and fervent pacifist, who had fallen out with his grandfather, the solitary, eleventh Duke, over his pacifism many years before and, therefore, hid from his son all knowledge of his inheritance. But the Duke's visits to

Woburn during his young days were protracted and on sufferance, and he never really got to know it.

Then his father was found shot on his estate of Endsleigh in Devon, and, in 1953, he became the thirteenth Duke.

When he took Woburn over it still retained all the coldness, the remote unhappiness it had been imbued with during his grandfather's day. Added to that was the desolation wrought by his father, who had unreasonably caused one of the wings to be pulled down and left the rest to fall into near-decay.

The new Duke and his Duchess, having decided at all costs to save Woburn and make it pay for itself by opening it to the public, worked like slaves to restore it. Any one of the millions of visitors it has received since can testify that they did a magnificent job. The Woburn the public sees is now fresh, welcoming and fascinating.

All this is common knowledge to anyone who has read the Duke's autobiography *A Silver Plated Spoon*, where it is most compellingly told. But what the Duke did not hint at was that "atmosphere" remained in the private wing—feelings and sensations which have refused to be removed by alterations and fresh paint.

Over tea in the white and gold library, he told us about the most obvious manifestation—a persistent and inveterate door-opener who had forced the Duke and his family out of what had once been their television room.

"It was convenient to find another television room anyway," the Duke told us, "because you had to pass through that one to get from one part of the wing to another. Nevertheless, the ghost became too inconvenient. You would be sitting there when suddenly one door would open—although nobody, as far as you could see, came in. Then, after a pause just long enough for someone to walk the length of the room, the door at the other end would open. And both doors would remain open. It wasn't frightening or anything, but it would take your mind off the programme, and it could get damned draughty.

"We did everything. We changed the locks—thinking they might be faulty. But it still happened, not all the time, but quite often. Then we kept the doors locked—and still they would open.

"Now we have reconstructed all that part of the wing, turning it into bedrooms and running a passage along it. So the place where the doors of the viewing-room used to be is now open passage.

"But the ghost seems to have changed its orbit because it now opens the communicating doors of the bedrooms. Someone who was staying with us mentioned it to me only the other day."

Then he added: "And then there are other things . . . further along the wing, in what is going to be a bedroom. They are more difficult to explain. They are not really concrete happenings . . . just rather nasty atmospheres, and they affect me a lot."

Thanks to the pulling down of the east wing, which had contained mainly guest bedrooms, the Duke inherited a home which ludicrously possessed thirty-two sitting rooms as opposed to eight bedrooms. However, most of the family's bedrooms remained, and the Duke converted these into flatlets.

At the tip of the southern wing and on the top floor are the airy rooms that were used as a bedroom by his grandparents and, later, himself. He decided to have them altered and redecorated as quarters for himself and his wife.

On our way there we called in on the haunted former TV room. Tom inspected it for a little, but said nothing to it, merely asking to be allowed to visit the other rooms. He felt that the spot was haunted, but that the cause of the trouble was sited further along the wing. So we went on.

In the proposed family quarters the light from a semi-circular window flooded the high rooms and turned to silver on the natural carved wood panelling, picking out the intricate pattern.

The Duke turned to Tom. "They aren't happy rooms, are they? I've spent a lot of time here in the past, and I propose to spend a lot of time here in the future, but there's still something about these rooms that is basically unhappy."

Tom agreed with him. "I think," he said, "that the whole trouble in this wing—your door-opening ghost—emanates from these rooms. I have the feeling that some-one was shut up in these rooms against their will."

That, as the Americans say, figured. The flinging open of doors would not be an inconsistent occupation for some-one who, during his lifetime, had been closed in by bars and bolts.

But, as Tom explained to us, there was more to it.

In his view the rooms had been soaked in unhappiness so much that it has accumulated over many lifetimes and distilled into one over-powering sense of general misery.

"I don't know what has happened here," he said, "but it has left an atmosphere so strong that it could be influential. I seriously advise you not to move into these rooms. I honestly believe they will make you unhappy."

It was the first time since our ghost hunts began that the mantle of Elijah had fallen on Tom. But, as he told me later, he felt the menace of that part of the wing so strongly that he had been obliged to warn against it.

"People don't realise what an influence like that can do," he said. "It cannot in itself alter people's lives, but it can bring out potentialities—turn arguments into quarrels, make a minor incident into a tragedy."

The Duke of Bedford remained unoffended. Tom had told him nothing that was inconsistent with the history of this part of the house.

Woburn, as a home for the Russells, got off to a bad start. It was given to the first Earl, John Russell, by the short-lived Edward VI, for services rendered to his father Henry VIII.

Like so many of the stately homes it had been a monastery, a Cistercian abbey, seized under the Dissolution in 1538. The Abbot had been brave enough to have spoken out publicly against Henry's marriage to Anne Boleyn. "It is a marvellous thing," he is supposed to have said, "that the King's grace could not be contented with that noble Queen, his very true and undoubted wife, Queen Katherine."

For that he was taken and hanged, with two of his monks, from the branches of the great oak tree which still stands in plain view before the south front of Woburn Abbey.

Inevitably, it is believed that he cursed Woburn as he died. Although the monastery was pulled down and a new house built, and even that, in the eighteenth century, was almost completely rebuilt, there are some who feel that the curse has come home to roost—albeit a little belatedly.

For, until the turn of this century, the Russells were one of the most powerful and influential families in England. They rose to this position, not because they were feudal aristocracy, but because they gave real service to the Crown as the new gentry.

By hard work and shrewd acquisition of land, they built up great estates and there was money in plenty. When, in 1641, Francis, the fourth Earl of Bedford died, his

"piggy bank"—a huge trunk—was found to contain
£1,557 14s. 1d. in cash. In the next twelve months, in the
days immediately preceding the outbreak of the Civil War,
his son William, later to be created the first Duke, poured
his income of £8,500 into it—a sum that would be worth
many times as much today. The income from his estates
in Devon and Cornwall alone was worth £2,500 then.

The Russells declared for Parliament during the Civil
War, and William became a general of the Roundheads—
among his officers was a captain named Oliver Cromwell—
and persisted in their puritan beliefs during the Restoration
that followed the Commonwealth. In fact, William's
eldest son, another William, was so incensed by Charles II's
Roman Catholic leanings that he got himself involved in
the Rye House Plot, was discovered and beheaded at
Lincoln's Inn Fields in 1683.

But in the face of even this tragedy the Russells managed
to keep on swelling the family coffers. The beheaded
William's father went on with the proposed marriage
between his orphan grandson to Elizabeth Howland,
heiress to much of the East India Company. The
bridegroom was fourteen years old and the bride thirteen. It was a match that was to bring tremendous wealth
and influence to the Russells of Woburn.

The Russells were a family who used their money wisely.
In 1630 they put about £100,000 into a scheme for drain-
ing the south fenlands around the Isle of Ely. It was a far-
sighted and eventually successful project which has made
the fenlands one of the best arable soils in England today.

A century later they invested in shipping to trade with·
India and were mainly responsible for the new docks at
Rotherhithe. At the end of the nineteenth century, when
the agricultural boom was at its height, we find them again
still very much in business and able to afford, like the good

landlords they were, to build spacious cottages with two or even three bedrooms each for their farm workers.

Then, in 1891, the ninth Duke who had been a great agriculturist, and M.P. for twenty-five years and a builder of some note, committed suicide in a fit of depression brought on by illness. His tragic death marked the turning point for the Russell family. From then on their fortunes went downhill. The three Dukes who succeeded him were all, in their various ways, both introverted and crankish, and their lives were marred by personal unhappiness—largely brought upon them by themselves.

The tenth Duke's marriage was an arranged one. His bride, the lovely, kind Lady Adeline Somers-Cocks, daughter of the third Earl of Somers, had had extreme pressure put on her by her mother, forcing her into this match with a man she did not love. It was a dismal, childless failure. The couple eventually ceased speaking to each other. At mealtimes they conversed through an intermediary. If ever there was anything important to be settled they would write notes to one another.

"My grandparents," said the Duke, "hid their troubles better. But they were never really in accord. My grandfather, Herbrand, was generous in giving to charity and in his dealings with his family and employees. He was a fine landlord and did a great deal for Woburn, but he was hopelessly unable to have a warm, human relationship with anyone. He and my grandmother followed separate interests and were polite, but distant to each other.

"I tried hard to become close to him when I found out that he was my grandfather, but I failed. When I heard of my grandmother's death I came rushing down to Woburn to see if I could help, but he showed no emotion even then, although her death must have hit him very hard."

60

The unhappiness that had descended over Woburn fell on the next generation. Herbrand's only child, Hastings—the present Duke's father—inherited his parent's inability to show love for anyone. He was just as isolated, cold, stubborn, and tragic a figure as his father. Probably because of the similarity in their personality, the two quarrelled violently and for twenty years they ignored each other's existence.

Hastings's marriage was very unhappy. Eventually the quarrel between him and his wife flared into the open and became the most publicised court case of 1935. A hopeless judge of public opinion, Hastings alienated most of the country by publicly declaring an admiration for Hitler, at a time when the tide of feeling in Britain was running strongly against Nazism.

During the thirteen years that he ruled Woburn, after his father's death in 1940, he wreaked havoc on the Abbey itself. One wing, a riding school, an ancient and beautiful tennis court and a museum were all needlessly demolished.

It was as if a malign Fate were pouring disaster and tragedy on Woburn, trying to counterbalance, in fifty years, for the prosperity and content it had got away with for three centuries. By the time the thirteenth and present Duke of Bedford inherited in 1953, the estate was on its knees. The double toll of death duties within a short space of time had left it financially crippled.

The unhappiness of the personal lives of its three succeeding generations left the Abbey's private apartments almost tangibly disturbed. The stock of the Russell family, formerly so high, had fallen in fifty years of bad public relations quite desperately low in the country.

Perhaps worst of all, the new Duke found that he was no longer master of his own estate. When, largely due to his efforts, his father and grandfather returned to speaking terms with each other, it was to make an arrangement that was to leave this, the thirteenth Duke, with his hands tied when he inherited.

Despite all this he has managed to restore Woburn to something of its former glory and do away with much of its loneliness. But the deep-rooted unhappiness experienced during the past fifty years in its private wing remains. The Duke knew it, and Tom Corbett knew it and had warned against it.

But I think that all of us, standing in that beautiful apartment realised that although the Duke of Bedford distrusted the atmosphere of those rooms, and had now had that distrust confirmed, he would not give them up. It was an ambivalence we were to find time and again in the stately home owners—an old, deep-rooted belief in the supernatural fighting with a modern disbelief in its influence.

The Duke of Bedford told us, for instance, that there were two rooms in the house which he found "restless". One was the Wood Library, the other was an office. It was so bad, he said, that he could not read for long in the one, nor work for any length of time in the other. Yet he continued to use both of them.

.   .   .   .   .

Outside, in Woburn Park, the public are allowed to roam the three thousand acres as freely as the deer. They can picnic beneath the trees and wander round the lakes.

It is significant that probably the only place in the grounds they are barred from is an isolated little summer-house standing on its own in the west side of the park, which the Duke feels is both haunted and unhappy. Its dark, overgrown garden is surrounded by a tall wooden fence and the gate is kept locked.

When the Duke took us there to stand in the centre of its small, circular room, Tom could find no specific ghost. "But it is a place where someone has done a lot of crying," he said.

To the Duke the little summer-house is haunted by his grandmother. "I feel her very strongly, every time I come here," he said. "We have a room devoted to her memory at the house, but for me she is here. Like so many of the Russell wives, she was unhappy at Woburn and hated the atmosphere there. She used to escape from it nearly every afternoon to come and sit here to think and be alone and write in her diary."

"The Flying Duchess", as she came to be called, met her future husband, Herbrand, the eleventh Duke of Bedford, in India. She received a frigid welcome from her parents-in-law—a beginning that was to make her feel unwanted at Woburn for the rest of her life.

When in 1891 she moved into Woburn as Duchess, she found that she was allowed no part either in the management of the house or in the upbringing of her own son. As compensation, she directed her considerable energy into other channels and horrified the polite society of those days by taking up nursing. Eventually she qualified as operations sister and radiographer. She opened a small cottage hospital at Woburn which became a model of its kind and assisted at most of the operations performed there and carried out all the radiography work herself. Deprived of human affection, she also lavished love on birds and animals, becoming a fine ornithologist.

As she grew older she became very deaf—but this did not stop her from taking up a new and, in those days, risky pastime—flying. In 1930, when she was sixty-four, she and a co-pilot made a record flight to South Africa and back, surviving a near crash when part of the plane caught fire, resulting in a forced landing in the jungle of Sudan.

But the great love of her life was for her hospital and when, a few years later, her husband told her she must give it up because it was proving too expensive, most of her enthusiasm for living was ended.

Sadly, she wrote: "I want a real rest, and fresh air and the birds and loneliness."

She took more and more to sitting in the isolation of her summer-house where she could watch her beloved birds undisturbed. Then one day, in 1937, she told everyone that she intended to complete her two hundred hours of solo flying. She had already put in one hundred and ninety-nine.

Her pilot mapped out a course for her which would take just an hour, and on March 22 she took off from a field at Woburn in her Gypsy aeroplane. She never returned. No part of her course should have taken her over the sea, but, six days later, after a frantic search, the wreckage of her plane was discovered—washed ashore on the east coast.

During her lifetime, she and her grandson had been kept apart by the restraint that Woburn seemed to impose on the entire family. After her death, however—which has always worried and troubled the Duke—he found among her papers a neatly-gathered, obviously treasured, collection of newspaper clippings, most of them from the society columns, which recorded his doings, his visits, the parties and balls he had attended when he was young. . . .

We did not stay long in the summer-house, and as we went the Duke carefully locked the gate behind him—leaving the secretive oasis to itself.

Outside in the park the crowds were streaming through the turnstiles, the children ran and shouted in the playground or milled about the tuck shop. The Duke of

Bedford regarded it with a mixture of pride and exasperation.

"All this," he said, "it will have to go on for ever. Even now the house is only just paying for itself. It costs £150,000 a year to keep up. You can't really be happy in a vast house like that. You don't run it, it runs you. There's nowhere you can escape from your problems. I hate the atmosphere in parts of it. But what can you do? Before I became Duke I used to avoid unhappy atmospheres as I avoided people I didn't like. Now I can't get away from them."

He looked around at the vast park and the huge, dominating house that rules it. "My wife and I are going to get a place away from all this and tell nobody where it is," he said. "Somewhere we can escape to now and then and I can leave the ghosts to get on with it."

He stood on the steps of Woburn to wave to us as we drove down the long drive. Then he turned and went back in..... to the ghosts that wouldn't leave him alone.

FOUR

Salisbury Hall

✳ ✳

FOUR MILES from St. Albans, as you approach it from London by the A6, there is a track leading off to the left. After rambling through a farmyard, the track suddenly becomes impressive, turns itself into a causeway bridge and leads over a moat on to a tiny island of lawns and trees which surround an old manor house.

This is Salisbury Hall, one of the smallest and least-known of the English stately homes. Yet 'for 1,000 years this tiny rectangle of land inside the moat, just seventy yards by sixty, has acted as a kind of lodestone, attracting to itself many of the great events and most of the great personalities that each passing century had to offer.

Write the history of Salisbury Hall and you write the history of England, beginning with the Romans. They probably used the spot as an outpost or signal station for St. Albans which can just be seen across the miles of flat, tilled fields that lie between.

There are records to substantiate that, in the year 800, the land was held by a Saxon, Asgar the Staller, whose title shows that he was a dignitary of some standing at court.

After the Norman invasion, the Conqueror gave it to his already immensely wealthy friend, Geoffrey de Mandeville.

It acquired its present name when, in 1380, Sir John Montagu, the Earl of Salisbury and a Knight of the Garter, married into it. Those were probably the Hall's greatest days when it belonged to men who ranked among the highest of England's chivalry.

It passed from Montagu to Nevill and was handed down to the most famous Nevill of them all, Warwick the Kingmaker. Both he and his younger brother, the Earl of Northumberland, were killed, practically on the Hall's doorstep, at the Battle of Barnet during the Wars of the Roses.

It fell into obscurity for a while until Sir John Cutte, Henry the VII's treasurer, found it and rebuilt it into a comfortable home in 1507. It was to stay in the Cutte family for two hundred and fifty years.

Charles I used Salisbury Hall as a headquarters and armoury during the Civil War and, in fact, in all of England's most important wars, this gentle Valhalla played a very active part. During the Second World War it was taken over lock stock and barrel by Sir Geoffrey de Havilland, amid great secrecy. It became a hush-hush establishment, surrounded by barbed wire and sentries, to which serious-looking men from London came and went.

It wasn't until late 1940 that the object of all this secrecy became known and then, from out of a hangar at the back of the house, trundled a revolutionary aeroplane, a combination of bomber and fighter, which was to help the Allies win the war. Sir Geoffrey de Havilland called it the Mosquito.

But out of all the history and pageantry of Salisbury Hall emerge two figures which, by sheer force of their personalities, command all the rest—a man and a woman who, at very different times and in extremely different ways, became household names.

67

The woman was Nell Gwynne and the man Sir Winston Churchill.

In 1668, that most charming of kings, Charles II, and that loveliest of fruit-sellers, Nell Gwynne, began their love affair—a liaison that was to last until the King's death sixteen years later. And in the same year, 1668, Salisbury Hall was purchased in mysterious circumstances.

It was owned at that time by a Richard Cole, of St. Martins in the Fields who, in 1617, had bought it for £3,100—a considerable amount of money in those days. Ostensibly its new buyer was a Mr. James Hoare, who paid Mr. Cole the inflated sum of £7,100 for it. Why such a large sum? Nobody believed that James Hoare wanted the place for himself. In fact, it is practically certain that he was buying it on behalf of the King who wanted it as an establishment for Mistress Eleanor Gwynne; somewhere for them to meet without offending the prying eyes at court.

Just one year after having laid out this fortune on the house, James Hoare transferred it to a fellow banker Jeremy Snow, a relation of Samuel Pepys. Now Snow was about the same age as the King and it is quite likely that he was his loyal friend and servant. It was probably part of the plan that, while ostensibly owning Salisbury Hall, Jeremy Snow and his wife Rebecca acted as discreet house-keepers and guardians for Charles.

It is known that Jeremy Snow, who later was rewarded with a baronetcy, carried out extensive alterations, raising the house to the standard demanded by a King and his mistress. Anyway, there still stands at Salisbury Hall a little oak-beamed cottage overlooking the Norman moat which is referred to as "Nell Gwynne's cottage". And in London Colney, the nearest village to the Hall, they still retell the legends of the time when she lived "up at the House".

They talk about the time when Charles granted Nell the right to levy a tax on every ton of coal brought within the London area. His only stipulation was that the area was to be one that she could travel round in a single day.

Mistress Nell's greed and wits made the best of the concession. She arranged for teams of fresh horses to be stationed in a wide radius around London, and rose at the crack of dawn to start travelling as far and as fast as she could.

She must have arrived back that night an extremely weary woman. But she had the satisfaction of knowing that her tax area covered several counties. The route she took now forms the boundary of the Metropolitan Police Area, a pear-shaped section which has its apex at London Colney.

It is a coincidence that the Chancellor of the Exchequer who was to compound these dues two centuries later was Sir Randolph Churchill, father of Winston, whose widow later came to live at Salisbury Hall.

It is to the Hall that Nell Gwynne is supposed to have brought her first child by the King. The legend goes that Nell, angling for a title for her son, said to Charles, "Throw the little bastard into the moat," and the King replied, "No, spare the first Duke of St. Albans." It seems likely when you think that there *is* a moat at Salisbury Hall, and the spires of St. Albans are there in the misty distance to inspire the title.

In 1905, the Hall saw a revival of its great days. The widowed Lady Randolph Churchill, the lovely Jenny, had married again—to a man much younger than herself, George Cornwallis-West—and she and her husband bought the house.

Every week-end the carriages of Edwardian society would roll noisily over the causeway. Melba, Duse and Edward VII himself were all visitors to the Hall.

But the most distinguished visitor was the man whose fame would top them all, Sir Winston Churchill, who as a young man sometimes stayed with his mother and step-father.

Sir Winston himself was unusually silent about that part of his life, maybe because he and his step-father, who was only a few years older than himself, did not get on too well. But his stay, whatever its length, was long enough to give rise to legends about the man in his own lifetime. In London Colney they still talk about the time he got rid of the huge pike that terrorised the moat by the individual method of shooting at it with a rifle.

In his day there used to stand a tall pollarded lime between the tennis courts and the daffodil beds—although it is not there now. For some reason grass would never grow around it. Now they explain that phenomenon by saying that Sir Winston used to find peace and quiet among its branches in which to write his most vitriolic speeches. Every time a piece of paper fluttered down to the ground, the words on it burnt the grass for ever. . . .

But there is a stronger link between Nell Gwynne and Sir Winston than the mere fact that both lived in the same house.

There is reason to believe that during the time the great man was staying there, the ghost of Nell Gwynne made at least one appearance, probably more. Sir Winston himself did not see it – he was not psychic. But his step-father did.

In a book that George Cornwallis-West wrote in 1930 (*Edwardian Hey-Days*. Putnams), he said that he had been very sceptical about anything to do with ghosts—until he went to live at Salisbury Hall. He devotes several pages to the incident that made him change his mind:

"One evening at Salisbury Hall just as it was getting dusk," he wrote, "I came down the staircase which leads into the old panelled room that we used as a dining-room, and there, standing in a corner, I saw the figure of a youngish and beautiful woman with a blue fichu round her shoulders. She looked intently at me, and then turned and disappeared through the door into the passage. I followed and found nothing.

"She looked so exactly like a former nursemaid of ours, called Ellen Bryan, an exceptionally lovely girl whom we, as children, for some quaint reason used to call 'Old Girlie' and who was then my mother's maid, that I felt certain she must have died and that I had seen an apparition of her at the moment of her death.

"Jack Churchill was living with us at the time, and I called him into the passage and told him about it. At his suggestion I rang up my mother at Newlands and after some conversation asked how 'Old Girlie' was; she replied that she was perfectly well and was going to marry a Quartermaster in the Artillery, so that disposed of my theory about the ghost.

"I thought no more about the matter until a few weeks later, when my sister Daisy came to visit us. As Salisbury Hall had been inhabited by Nell Gwynne, I had made a hobby of collecting prints of this lady, most of which were in the library, and taking up one, Daisy said: 'I never realised before the truth of what people used to say about Old Girlie'.

"I asked her what she meant, and she replied: 'Don't you remember they used to say she was exactly like the pictures of Nell Gwynne?'

"For the first time I realised the possibility of my having seen the apparition of the former mistress of Salisbury Hall.

"A few days later I mentioned it to a friend who was a member of the psychic Research Society, who begged me to write a letter which she could put into the hands of a medium, in order that some light might be thrown on the mystery.

"I was still sceptical, but, after some persuasion wrote the letter. Three weeks later I heard from my friend that it had been placed in the hands of a medium who had stated that the writer had seen 'an apparition of Mistress Eleanor Gwynne, who had come to warn him against an impending danger'.

"I knew of no impending danger at the time; but within six months of my having seen the apparition a solicitor to whom I had entrusted a large sum of money to pay off some mortgages, absconded and let me in for over ten thousand pounds."

.   .   .   .   .

As Tom, Jeremy Grayson, the photographer, and I drove down the track we knew very litttle of the Hall's history and nothing at all about its ghosts—next to nothing has been written about the house, and what little literature there is proves extremely difficult to find.

The reply to my letter by Mr. Walter Goldsmith, the present owner, had said merely that he would be pleased to receive Mr. Corbett and myself and that there were "several ghosts" for us to investigate.

We found Mr. Goldsmith, a painter and art dealer, in his shirtsleeves working on his self-appointed and back-breaking job of restoring the Hall to something of its past glory.

When, in 1956, he and his wife had found it and fallen in love with it, the house and grounds were in a terribly neglected condition—still carrying most of the scars of the De Havilland occupation.

Tom asked Mr. Goldsmith that, as a kind of psychic

Tom Corbett in Mary Tudor's bed at Sawston Hall

The Marquis of Bath in the Red Library at Longleat

The corner of the Red Library where the eighteenth-century ghost is seen

exercise, he should be told nothing of Salisbury Hall's ghosts, but be allowed to discover them for himself.

He found Nell Gwynne almost right away.

We had crossed the black and white Jacobean floor of the Crown Chamber beneath which lie Tudor and Norman floors, climbed up Sir Jeremy Snow's staircase and entered the first upstairs room, the cool Green Bedroom, when Tom called a halt.

Quietly we all waited.

"You have two ghosts here," said Tom.

"Yes."

"A man and a woman."

"Yes."

"The woman is very beautiful and somewhere in the house you have a portrait of her."

"Yes."

Then—and not until then—Mr. Goldsmith told us the legend of Nell Gwynne's stay at the house and how, two-and-a-half centuries later, Cornwallis-West saw her with her blue fichu round her shoulders standing at the bottom of the staircase.

At other times, other people have seen her, either on the stairs or near the Green Bedroom in which we were standing.

"I am glad that you detected her in here," Mr. Goldsmith told Tom. "There is no foundation for it, but in my own mind I always think of this room as the 'haunted bedroom'. I always sense that there is someone in here."

He took us downstairs into the flagged Hallway to show us the gold-framed portrait of Nell Gwynne that is hanging there. It shows her dressed in her favourite blue, looking very beautiful with her blonde curls ornately dressed.

"As a confirmation of what I have told you," said Tom

73

definitely. "You are one day going to receive a much larger portrait of her."

The clairvoyancy he possesses, which works backwards and forwards, had taken a brief jump into the future. I am quite sure that one day I shall revisit Salisbury Hall to find a large portrait of Nell Gwynne hanging in the Crown Chamber. And Mr. Goldsmith expects its arrival daily.

As to Tom's "man", Mr. Goldsmith told us that in an old book on the house he had found a reference to a cavalier who had died a grisly death at the Hall and whose ghost, in those days, was frequently seen.

"Sometimes he appeared with a sword sticking through him. Other people said it was obvious he had shot himself. None of us have seen him. But we have one more ghost for you. . . ." And we continued our tour.

When Mr. and Mrs. Goldsmith had installed themselves and their four children at the Hall, it was a very different house to the great mansion it had been in Tudor days. The lovely wing that Sir John Cutte had built had been pulled down by nineteenth-century vandals. As a compensating factor, however, a hideous Edwardian addition of a ballroom at the back of the house had also gone. The house was badly in need of repair and its wood was rotting. "Another year," said Mr. Goldsmith, "and it would probably have been too late to save it."

Depleted and drab as it then was, the Goldsmiths found themselves increasingly captivated by the house and its history. They began a long and complicated search among old books, manuscripts and records to find references to the Hall. They found that, previously unknown to them, the house was a labyrinth of secret passages, sliding panels and hidden rooms.

Acting upon the information they winkled out from old documents, books, records and diaries, they uncovered glorious tiled fireplaces that had been bricked in. They found hidden recesses in the dark panelling of the hall.

Continuing the historical detective work, they found a secret passage at the back of the cupboard in one of the top floor bedrooms that led, rather suggestively, into another bedroom. They discovered a completely hidden room under the eaves—probably a priest's hiding hole.

"The one thing we haven't done," said Mr. Goldsmith, "is to open up the old cellars. We located the entrance, but we haven't yet been able to investigate them because of the amount of rubble blocking the way in.

"I have great hopes of them when we do. Apart from priceless old wine, I have reason to believe that in the thirteenth century the Earl of Salisbury blocked up some medieval statues in there, when the cellars were a crypt to the chapel. If I'm right those statues would be extremely rare."

Best of all, Mr. Goldsmith found that he could hardly dig a spade into the earth around the house without coming up with some archaeological treasure. A glass case in his drawing room contains some of his finds—rare, ancient coins, a human thigh bone and the fourteenth-century spur that was lying near it.

In his efforts to bring the visual history of the Hall right up to date, Mr. Goldsmith asked De Havilland if the prototype of the Mosquito fighter-bomber might be allowed to stay where it was built, in the hangar in the back garden.

They gave their permission, and visitors to the Hall can see it, standing in the hangar looking fresh and lethal, but already a relic of a past age in flying.

"I believed in ghosts before I came to Salisbury Hall," Mr. Goldsmith told us, "but once I had moved in the belief became stronger. I was sure the house was haunted.

"In my studio on the top floor I felt a presence, warm and friendly, but a supernatural presence.

"I've found out since that it was in that room that an inexplicable bloodstain used to appear and re-appear on the wall—but I've never found it.

"My wife, now, was extremely sceptical about ghosts. She didn't believe in them. Yet she was the one who experienced hearing one when we got here.

"Upstairs there is a room where our sons sleep. It has a little tiny dressing-room leading off it over the porch and it is on the left side of the house where the Tudor wing used to adjoin.

"They mentioned more than once they thought it was haunted and that something used to pass their door in the night. They took it completely in their stride—children do."

Mrs. Audrey Goldsmith told us what had happened to her. "The boys were away and, as I was ill at the time, I had moved into their room for a bit. This particular night I had been unable to go to sleep and was awake about 2 a.m., reading a book. I was quite alert.

"Then I heard these unmistakable footsteps in the passage outside my door. The passage, which now ends in the bathroom, once led into the old Tudor wing that was destroyed in 1818.

"I presumed the footsteps to be those of my husband, as everyone else was away, and was quite expecting to see him open my door as he would see the light underneath it, and know I was awake. However, the footsteps passed on but did NOT return.

"The next morning I said that I had heard him go to the bathroom, and he told me he had slept all night without stirring.

"Some time afterwards we received a visit from the

daughter of Sir Nigel Gresley, who lived here between 1934 and 1939. She asked me whether I had heard the ghost. She said that guests, who in their day were put in the large red bedroom, were always troubled by strange footsteps in the night.

"Now this is interesting because it was a different room from the one I was in when I heard the ghost. I believe that it is the passage that is haunted, rather than any one room. Anyway, I have changed my mind about ghosts since we've come to live here. Too many people seem to have heard the one that I did.

"In 1959, quite out of the blue came a letter from a woman in Bangkok who had lived at Salisbury Hall when she was a child. She had read a magazine article about the house and all we had done for it and the memories of the happy times she had here came flooding back, and she wrote us this wonderful letter. The amazing thing is that she confirms the haunting in the part of the house where I heard it."

Mr. and Mrs. Goldsmith have kindly lent me this very charming letter from Mrs. Rosamund Stutzel so that I can quote the apposite passage:

"There was far too little, for my taste, in the article about the ghosts and legends . . . and I would like to tell you some of those we knew in those days. You may know them all and I hope you do.

"One ghost, often felt by the children, was in the bedroom over the entrance hall, with the porch dressing-room. This was my parents' room and a child used to sleep at the foot of the bed.

"Both my small brother and my sister were wakened by 'something' standing by the bed, and this on many occasions.

77

"In this same room my governess spent a night while my mother was away on business, but she would never sleep another night in the house as, she said, 'something terrifying came out of the wall near the fireplace and stood by the bed.' Another friend had the same experience.

"And in the 1919 'flu my mother became more and more ill until moved out of that room. It is interesting to speculate that the house looks cut off and as though there should be other rooms just where the ghost used to come out of the wall."

The letter ends: "Thank you for saving the house from ruin. You seem to have been led to it in the nick of time."

Tom went over the house carefully, but was unable to find any ghost other than the two he had already described, the one that was presumably a cavalier, and Nell Gwynne. One of those two, he said, was responsible for the footsteps in the passage. He believed it was the man, and that he emanated from the missing Tudor wing. He did not believe him to be harmful in any way. "It is doubtful if the mother would get better when her sleep was being disturbed every night," he said. "I don't think this ghost is exerting any ill influence."

This raised an aspect of ghosts that I, for one, had not encountered before—their disregard of modern conditions. It is not always the case, of course, but very often it seems that a ghost who haunted a building which has since disappeared either refuses to accept that it has gone or believes that it still exists. Before 1818 there was a free passage leading from the Tudor wing to the older centre section. The Tudor wing has gone, and a brick wall blocks thin air from what remains of the passage in the centre section, but the ghost plods on blindly from carpeted passage, through the brick wall and on into space, two storeys up in the air, and then back again.

Lord Christopher Thynne, the son of the Marquess of Bath, who had shared our night's vigil at Longleat, told me that during a tour of America recently he visited a country newspaper office. While he was there he was shown the most amazing photograph that had been taken by one of the newspaper's photographers in an old colonial house.

"The photographer had gone to take shots of the house purely to illustrate an article about it," said Lord Christopher. "The idea that it was haunted had not entered his head. But when he got back to the office and developed the negatives he was amazed to see that on one of them was the hazy, but unmistakable figure of a woman. As he had been alone in the room, there was no doubt that he had photographed a ghost. But what clinched the matter was that the woman appeared to be standing on her knees. The bottom half of her legs seemed cut off. When the newspaper investigated they found that the modern owners of the house had raised the floor level of that room about a foot. The ghost was standing on the floor that had existed when she was alive."

There is no good explanation for these ghostly anachronisms. Tom Corbett has never pretended that his brief glimpses behind the veil that divides us from the fourth dimension have given him any insight into its exact workings. It is obvious, of course, that time moves at a different tempo for ghosts, but just how and why is not at all clear.

However, after our visits to four very haunted houses, Littlecote, Longleat, Woburn and now Salisbury Hall, a picture of the typical, average ghost—if there is such a thing—was beginning to acquire a little shape. Some of the maleficence it had taken on for me after Longleat and

79

Woburn was fading and in its place it was assuming the pathos of a trapped animal. Any entity that chooses to spend centuries pacing floors that are no longer there, for reasons that everyone but itself has forgotten, is too sad to be frightening.

I was rather sorry to find Nell Gwynne, a character for whom I have always had a sneaking affection, in such company. However, her appearances have not been made so often—she has not been seen since 1905, although she is still sufficiently there to be traced by Tom—nor so senselessly as the poor cavalier's.

As we left Salisbury Hall, we visited the little cottage which overlooks the moat by the bridge and which to this day is called "Nell Gwynne's cottage". It is now a "factory" where silk-worms produce fine-quality silk. It was from here that the silk came for Queen Elizabeth's wedding dress and coronation gown.

For a long time we stood chatting with Mr. Goldsmith, looking into the moat where Winston Churchill shot his pike. I think that we were reluctant to leave the charm and quiet of Salisbury Hall for the noise and smell of the A6.

Suddenly Tom began pacing the causeway bridge, his hands behind his back, his head on one side, as if judging its length. Mr. Goldsmith looked at him, puzzled, but Jeremy and I, who knew the signs by now, just waited.

Eventually Tom said quietly: "Don't ever be surprised if someone sees a ghost on this bridge. There is a woman here. Again, I can't put a date to her. That is always terribly difficult to do. But you don't have to worry about her. Like the other ghosts in the house, she means no harm."

Mr. Goldsmith didn't look worried. Anything—natural or supernatural—that will enhance his beloved Salisbury Hall is all right by him.

FIVE

Sawston Hall

IT IS SAD, but true, that more of England's stately homes have been spoilt by their owner's wealth than by any other factor. It has enabled them to indulge in any whims and fashions of architecture that each passing century dictated, so that their unfortunate descendants now find themselves living in houses that run the architectural gamut from medievalism to Victoriana.

Sawston Hall, near Cambridge, was saved from this fate by the fact that the Huddlestons, who have owned it for four and a half centuries, have had to pay dearly for their religious constancy for the last four of them.

When, towards the latter end of the sixteenth century, the tide in England turned against Catholicism, the Huddlestons refused to turn with it and clung to the old faith. During the persecution, torture and fines that came to the Catholics at the accession of Elizabeth and for long after, the family remained persistently Catholic, and therefore persistently liable to fines—only their courage and tenacity keeping their heads high and above water level. They were left with just enough money to maintain their home, but not sufficient to alter it structurally, with the result that Sawston is now as perfectly complete and unspoilt as the day it was built.

Along with Salisbury Hall—both houses at one time

belonged to John Nevill, the Kingmaker's younger brother—I rank it as one of the most charming houses in England. There is a greater sense of period here than almost anywhere else, a closer rapport with the past and the stubborn, charming men and women who were part of it.

Upstairs, in the haunted section of Sawston Hall, there is a steady stream of unexplained movements, sounds and mysteries. I shall deal with these, and what Tom Corbett, after a night in the haunted bedroom, decided caused them, later in the chapter. Apart from these recurrent happenings there are other ghosts—long-dead Huddlestons who, during the lifetime of the previous owner, the late Captain Eyre-Huddleston and his wife, have broken through the barrier to flash across the scene of their old home.

Mrs. Clare Huddleston, the Captain's wife and a granddaughter of a former Duke of Norfolk, came to Sawston as a bride in 1930 and often heard the sound of a spinet being played. "The first time," she said, "I was standing in the hall at the foot of the stairs, and I heard this music quite distinctly. The only musical instrument we had in the house was the old harpsichord, and I knew it wasn't that. The tone was much lighter. Besides, there was nobody playing the harpsichord.

"When Captain Huddleston came home I told him what had happened. He didn't believe in ghosts in those days, and he said, 'Nonsense.'

"But then, some time later, a friend of mine who was staying with us, said, 'What is that tinkly music I keep hearing?' "

Mrs. Huddleston smiled at her husband. "That stopped him," she said. "I used to hear the spinet quite often after that. It never frightened me, although I knew it was supernatural. It was very lovely. But I haven't heard it now for many years."

Captain Huddleston's scepticism had softened over the years. A magistrate for over twenty years, he was used to weighing evidence, and the evidence of ghosts at Sawston presented to him at various times by his family and friends had at last brought from him the admission, "I'm perfectly certain that an influence exists which some people feel and others don't."

Which is, after all, a pretty fair summing up of the supernatural situation.

The case for ghosts had been considerably strengthened when the present owner Major Eyre, the Captain's nephew, was helping prepare the house for its opening to the public.

He was alone at Sawston, in the hall, waiting for the arrival of the young ladies who were going to act as guides for the tourists. Suddenly, a sound rang through the house, floating downstairs from the upper floor. But this was not a spinet. This, quite unmistakably, was the trill of a girl's laughter.

Major Eyre wondered if, perhaps, any of the guides had arrived without their approach being noticed, and went in search of them. But the house was deserted and not until some time later did the girls arrive. It had been a ghost.

There are less cheering ways of being haunted than by music and laughter, but the ghosts that caused them have gone again and, although he went over the whole house carefully, Tom was unable to find a trace of them.

The happiness that gave rise to such pleasant haunting, however, remains secure between Sawston's walls. Despite the persecution of centuries—or perhaps because of it— the Huddlestons have always been a close, united family who created their own contentment and kept it fast to themselves.

. . . . .

The Parish of Sawston is older than England. Flints have been found there which show that it was a caveman settlement. The Romans had an outpost there, the Anglo-Saxons had a village, and a manor that stood where the Hall is now is mentioned in the Domesday Book as being surrounded by 600 acres of farmland.

In 1377 that manor became the property of Sir Edmund de la Pole, Captain of Calais during the war with France and Sheriff of Cambridgeshire and Huntingdonshire.

Through the female line it became the property of the Nevills, and when the youngest of the beautiful Nevill sisters married William Huddleston, a descendant of the Sir Richard Huddleston who had fought with Henry V at Agincourt, Sawston Hall was given to her as her portion of the estates.

Glory—and trouble—came to the hitherto quiet Sawston on July 7, 1553. John Huddleston and his wife Bridget were "at home", unaware that great forces were gathering which were to destroy their peace. Unknown to them—and indeed unknown to almost everyone in England—the consumptive, fifteen-year-old Edward VI had died a few days previously in Greenwich Palace. His ruthless and ambitious adviser, the Duke of Northumberland had thrown a double cordon of guards round the Palace to stop the news from leaking out, and had seized the armoury in the Tower.

Mary Tudor, the unhappy "Bloody" Mary, was now rightful Queen of England. But she, as ignorant of her brother's death as the rest of England, was hurrying down to London from Hunsdon in Hertfordshire to be at Edward's sickbed. All Northumberland had to do was to wait until she arrived, put her in the Tower and declare Lady Jane Grey, the poor doomed girl he had hastily married off to his son, Guildford Dudley, as Queen.

To hurry his plan along and make assurance doubly sure, however, he sent another son, Robert, later to be one of Elizabeth's favourites, at the head of a troop of cavalry to intercept and capture Mary. But Northumberland had misjudged the temper of England—an error that was to cost him his head—and sympathisers managed to warn Mary before Robert Dudley could get to her.

By that time she had reached Hoddesdon. Immediately she and her small group of attendants wheeled round and started for Kenninghall in Norfolk to rally her supporters.

Among her gentlemen was Andrew Huddleston, and it was at his suggestion that Mary turned off the road north to get shelter for the night at Sawston. No doubt she needed the rest, but the delay was very nearly fatal.

We don't know John's reaction when his royal guest came riding up out of the evening. But we do know his reaction when, a few hours later, a message came saying that Dudley was on the scent and rapidly bearing down on Sawston. He woke the Queen who was sound asleep in her four-poster—the bed is still at Sawston and Tom Corbett was to sleep in it four hundred years later—and had his women, so says tradition, dress her as a milkmaid. Mass was said right away and within minutes Mary left the house, travelling pillion behind a manservant, with John Huddleston in attendance.

At a vantage point they looked back to see if the pursuers were at the house. They saw that they had not only arrived there but, furious at losing their prey, had set fire to it.

Mary, so the story goes, said, "Let it blaze. When I am Queen I'll build Huddleston a better house."

With the odds at that moment against her ever becoming

Queen, and an even chance that not only she, but her helpers, would be beheaded, the promise must have seemed rather an empty one to poor John as his old moated manor crackled away. But Mary made it good. Some of the house was still standing after the fire and, with Queen Mary's permission, it was rebuilt with the stones from Cambridge Castle.

The Queen also rewarded Huddleston with a knighthood and appointed him Vice-chamberlain at Court and Captain of Philip's body-guard. He lived to enjoy them for only four years. In 1558, a year after Sir John's death, Mary died. The great reign of Elizabeth began, and with it came trouble for the Catholic families like the Huddlestons. . . .

It is the people of that new house and that new age who seem so close to you at Sawston now. The Hall is almost exactly the same today as it was then, even down to the furniture and the formal garden. It is not easy for twentieth-century minds to fathom the nature of the people who lived even four hundred years ago. Nevertheless, a walk through Sawston Hall can tell you a lot.

What dominated their lives, of course, was their loyal adherence to their faith and its punishing consequences. By 1573, Sir John's widow, Bridget, had been forced to hide out at the house of her daughter, Lady Lovell, in Norfolk, in order to avoid arrest. Her son Edmund and his children remained behind, to suffer the fines and confiscations that followed.

The cruellest cut of all came when the Elizabethan state passed a law enforcing the compulsory attendance of everyone at the new Protestant Sunday service. Down in Cornwall, a Catholic gentleman of this time, John Trevelyan, would satisfy the law by attending the reading of the lesson and the singing of the hymns, and then satisfy his own conscience by ostentatiously walking out at the beginning of the sermon. But at Sawston, the 23-year-old grand-daughter of John Huddleston, Jane, absolutely refused to attend the church at all.

A symbol of the fear the family lived in at Sawston during those long years is the Priests' Hiding Hole, a superbly-hidden little room, just big enough for one man and built into the tower. It was designed and built by Nicholas Owen, the great Catholic craftsman, whose work remains to this day in many of the Catholic houses and which saved so many priests from discovery and execution. More than one Jesuit, who risked his life going about the country, celebrating the forbidden mass, hid in Sawston's Hole while a search was made for him by the Queen's followers.

It is hidden in the thickness of the wall and its trap door is part of the floorboards of a tiny, ill-lit landing. When Major Eyre pointed it out to me, I was standing on top of it—and still couldn't see it.

Jane Huddleston—the same Jane who so steadfastly refused to attend Protestant services—had married a Mr. Wiseman, of Broadoaks in Essex, another Catholic house with a hiding hole. There was a continual traffic of priests between the two houses of Sawston and Broadoaks and almost every week Jane was risking her life by harbouring them. She was walking a tightrope, and she knew it. Finally it snapped and she was arrested. For her "crimes" and for refusing to give evidence against the priests, she was condemned to be pressed to death—one of the most dreadful forms of death that even that age had to offer.

Elizabeth, however, was touched by the girl's youth and courage and the sentence was commuted to one of life imprisonment. When the Queen died, Jane was released from prison by James I.

The Huddleston's faithful steward, John Rigby, however, did not get off so lightly. He had travelled to London to answer for his lady, was convicted of the same offence and hanged and quartered.

In 1605, Jane's brother, Henry, followed her example of defiance and became involved in the Gunpowder Plot. He was tried before the Chief Justice, acquitted, but forfeited some of his Essex lands as a recusant.

But despite the constant fear and alarms, life went on. The Huddlestons had no money to spare for grand alterations, but they did manage to keep up with the times. In fact, they were probably ahead of their time in many ways. They were one of the first families to install that last word in Tudor luxury—a lavatory chute, which was a large pipe running down the outside of the house from the attic to the garden.

And as the ladies swished up and down the Long Gallery, taking their exercise on rainy days, they were able to look out at the garden through panes of the new-fangled glass.

They played the spinet and laughed with enough force and pure enjoyment to make it echo down the centuries. They wrote prodigious letters to one another—most of them now preserved in the valuable Sawston collection, the first dating from 1579—swapping news and recipes.

Mrs. Huddleston had found one glorious recipe for a medicine among the old letters in the house. The sender claimed that it had cost "two hondered pounds". The recipe reads: "Take Venice Turpentine four pounds, Olibanum, Mastick, of each two ounces, Benjamin, Labdenum, Castoreum, Aloes, Hepattica, Date-stones, Dasy roots, Bettany roots, Cumfry roots of each one ounce. Powder all these, mingle them and distill them in a glass body and head in the sand. First a white Oyl will come over, then yellow, then Red, which keep apart, as also keep the waters apart as they come over.

"It cures Impostumes, Ulcers, Fistules, Cold Swelling, Bruises, Aches, Hemroydes, Appoplexi, Palsy pains, Contractures, Asthmas or stiffling of ye lungs in venom humors. It preserveth youth and recovereth most diseases. When the bell tolls for the dying patient, anoynt with it outwardly, or give twenty drops in a spoonful of Canary. And farther, it provoks sweat, expells poyson, it stayeth immoderate Courses, healeth pissing of blood, cleanseth ye kidneys and the wombe, advanceth Conception, takes away Crudities in ye stomach and cures obstructed spleens. Outwardly it heals cutts, wounds, bruises, old ulcers, fistules with corrupt bones which makes it to scale, it dissolveth hard swellings and tumors left incurable."

Another, equally venomous-sounding recipe, called the Duke of Portland's Receipt to Cure the Gout, said sagely: "As this Medicine operates insensibly, it will perhaps take two years before ye benefit ye receive from it be very great."

The Huddlestons had need of all the medicines they could get, for the Civil War was looming up and, once more, they were to be on the losing side. Even when Charles II was restored to the throne he was unable to do much to ease the suffering of families like the Huddlestons. He was watched like a hawk by his Protestant Parliament. He did, however, stand firm on exempting Father John Huddleston, a cousin of the Sawston family and a Benedictine monk, from the order which banished all Roman Catholic priests from the country. Father Huddleston had helped to save the King from capture after the Battle of Worcester, and was with him when he died.

Among the later Huddleston letters, circa 1800, there is one written by Jane Huddleston, the great-great-aunt of

Captain Huddleston, who was the delightful family historian of her time. This particular letter is worth mentioning because it comes within the province of the supernatural. In it, Jane is all agog at the strange happenings in the house of the village tanner, which was setting Sawston by the ears.

The letter was to her nephew, Richard, who was then the commanding officer of the Cambridgeshire Regiment, and tells with dramatic detail how the tanner's wife, on entering a particular room in the house, was mysteriously seized by an unseen force, her dress ripped off her and left in tatters. According to Jane, who was baffled by this and made searching inquiries, there was no rational explanation and it happened more than once.

Tom Corbett believes that the tanner and his wife must have had an adolescent son or daughter in the house at the time, for the "unseen force" was obviously a poltergeist.

Poltergeists, incidentally, are *not* ghosts. They are a mischievous and sometimes malevolent energy, almost always caused by the presence of a child which has just reached puberty—a kind of elemental force that is unconsciously thrown off by the child.

However, to return to the real ghosts. . . .

.   .   .   .   .

With a kindness that is typical of them, Captain and Mrs. Huddleston had asked Tom Corbett, myself and Jeremy Grayson, to spend the night at Sawston. Tom had begged them over dinner to tell him nothing about Sawston's main ghost before he had an opportunity of passing judgement on it. So, when the Huddlestons retired at eleven, leaving us to go where we pleased, we had no idea of what we were expected to see or hear.

Tom had been put in the Tapestry Bedroom which, we

knew from a modest little sentence in the brochure, was "supposed to be haunted". It is a big chamber hung from ceiling to floor with Flemish tapestries of Bible scenes. Its focal point is Queen Mary's bed, the elegant, canopied four-poster, in which she spent her disturbed night, on July 7, 1553. A door near the head of the bed led into the Panelled Bedroom, another led into the Little Gallery.

My bedroom led directly on to the old oak staircase; Jeremy's was further along a little passage nearby.

Tom mapped out his plan of campaign to the two of us —acting on his theory that ghosts are at their best, or worst, between the hours of midnight and 2 a.m., we still had an hour to wait for anything to happen.

"At midnight we will wander round, concentrating on the Tapestry Bedroom and the top of the staircase outside Diana's room," he said. "I feel those are productive areas."

"Thank you very much," I said.

"Until then," went on Tom, who is an inveterate card player, "we will sit in my room and have a few hands of gin rummy."

Obediently, I followed Tom out into the hall, Jeremy bringing up the rear, and went upstairs. At the top of the stairs, outside my room, Tom turned to say something to Jeremy—but Jeremy wasn't there.

"I thought Jeremy came up with us," said Tom, slowly.

"So did I," I said.

From downstairs Jeremy's voice floated up to tell us that he was gathering together his camera equipment and would join us in a few minutes.

"But I *heard* him," said Tom. "I heard his footsteps coming up behind us."

I hadn't heard any footsteps, but the impression that

91

someone was following me up had been so strong that I had never doubted Jeremy was behind me.

"Well," said Tom, rubbing his hands, "it looks like being a good night for ghosts."

One hour later, after Tom had taken 14p off me and 20p off Jeremy, we began the hunt proper.

A ghost hunt with Tom Corbett is an experience never to be forgotten. As I have tried to show, he abhors the dramatic mumbo-jumbo adopted by so many of his colleagues. His method is to walk quietly through rooms and corridors, usually with his hands in his pockets. Yet at every step he is picking up supra-natural vibrations like a cat picks up currents of scent. And something of this keen awareness is thrown off on his companions. I, for one, became alive to every draught, every movement in the still house. My imagination sharpened too, and the Huddlestons of long ago crowded about, whispering.

"There is a presence around," said Tom. "I can't put a sex to it yet, but it is kind. I don't seem able to pin it down, though.

"Come on," he said to me. "We'll all go and sit in your room and see if anything comes up those stairs again."

We sat just inside my door watching the stairs for a good half hour, silent, aware of the house around us. At the end of that time, Tom gave up.

"It's no good," he said. "I don't think we'll find anything now, we might just as well go to our beds."

"The trouble with ghosts," he added bitterly as he said good night, "is that they have no sense of what's fitting."

At times there are great comforts to be derived from knowing one is not psychic. I heartened myself with the fact that if a ghost came up and howled in my ear, I was not tuned in to the necessary wavelength to hear it. It was amazing what a sense of menace my room took on, though, once I was left to myself. I became uncomfortably conscious of the yawning staircase outside the door. But if journalism has given me nothing else, it has at least taught me to perfect the great art of going to sleep anywhere, at any time, under all circumstances, and the next time I thought about anything, it was morning. . . .

Tom was late joining us all at breakfast, and when he did arrive he looked very tired. He had found his ghost all right.

"I have had a very fatiguing night," he said to Captain and Mrs. Huddleston. "Your ghost has woken me every hour on the hour since four o'clock.

"I have an alarm clock, a very good alarm clock, which I set for 7 a.m. when I went to bed last night. It went off at four, although it was still set for seven, and I woke up to find someone was fiddling with the latch of the door. The alarm went off again at five; again, the alarm hand was still pointing to seven, and I heard someone prowling around the Panelled Room behind me. The same thing happened at six, and again I had the sense of someone checking my room."

He turned to Captain Huddleston. "Do you know what I think your ghost is? A night watchman. It is definitely a man and it is definitely protective. I should imagine he was employed as watchman here once, and has now taken the job of looking after the house at night, seeing that no harm comes to it. There's no harm in him.

"At one point a word which sounded like 'Cutlass' kept flashing into my mind. I think it was the ghost's name. Does it mean anything to you?"

Mrs. Huddleston shook her head. She had never heard of a man called Cutlass. But the rest, she told us, made sense.

The theory about a night watchman was a new idea, but

it certainly fitted the facts; was, indeed, almost the only feasible explanation.

"When we first came to Sawston," began Mrs. Huddleston. "The Tapestry Room was supposed to be haunted by one of those inevitable Ladies in Grey.

"A retired maid who served here during the last part of the last century told me that there were always three long knocks on the door, which would then open and a grey shape float across the room. She said she had been kneeling down setting the fire there one morning when it had happened to her. She actually saw this 'grey thing' pass by her.

"She was so frightened she ran out of the room into the Little Gallery and fell down the steps which lead into it, hurting herself badly. But if there ever was a Grey Lady, she had certainly gone by the time we arrived. There was no doubt, though, that something was haunting up there— and not only the Tapestry Room but the Panelled Bedroom and *your* room"—she nodded at me—"as well. We don't use those bedrooms ourselves, but as we are short of rooms we often have to put guests into them, and time and again our guests have come down to breakfast to tell about someone coming to their door in the middle of the night.

"There was Father Martindale, a well-known priest, who came to stay and I put him in the room Mrs. Norman had last night. The next morning he told us he had had a terribly disturbed night and that periodically there had been someone rapping on his door. The Father was sure it was a ghost.

"Then a young married woman friend of mine came to stay in the same room and the following day she said: 'There's a ghost up there, isn't there?'

"I asked her why she thought so, and she said: 'Oh, I always know when there's a ghost about—my arms go all goose-pimply, and that's how they went last night'."

Mrs. Huddleston gave us instances of how knocks and noises had been heard coming from the Panelled Room when it was unoccupied, and went on:

"Not so long ago, a young undergraduate came to stay. Again I was short of room, so I put him in Queen Mary's bed in the Tapestry Room. He had a bad cold, I remember, and I had dosed him up well. The next morning he came down to breakfast looking as if something strange had happened—we're getting used to our guests looking like that.

"Halfway through breakfast, he said to me, 'It was kind of you to look in on me last night, but you needn't have bothered—I was perfectly all right.'

"I exclaimed that I didn't know what he was talking about. 'Last night,' he said, 'you looked into my room to see how I was. I know you did.'

"I assured him that I hadn't, which made him a bit scared. He explained that he had heard somebody on the steps outside his room. It had woken him up in the small hours. Then somebody had knocked on the door. He said 'Come in' and there was a fiddling at the latch, but no one went in. He said 'Come in' again, but nobody did, so he got frightened and put his head under the bedclothes and eventually went to sleep."

The similarity between the experiences of Father Martindale, the undergraduate and Tom Corbett was striking. In each case the three men had felt that there was someone at their door.

And two of them had felt it was protective—the undergraduate assumed it was Mrs. Huddleston "seeing if he was all right" while Tom described it as "checking".

Once again, without knowing any of the previous experiences, Tom had supplied an explanation which, on inspection, was both reasonable and likely.

Anybody who has studied ghosts has found that love for a house or its inmates can be just as strong a pull to a spirit as hatred. It is a fact, too, that the Huddlestons have always been able to inspire great loyalty and affection in their servants (witness the sacrifice of John Rigby). So why should not an old servant still be blindly carrying on his duty long after his death? He cannot check up on the present generation because they now sleep in rooms which were not in use in his day. But he can protect the rooms he knows.

.   .   .   .   .

As, I think, I have made clear, it never occurs to me to doubt any of Tom Corbett's pronouncements on what the ghosts are and why they are doing what they are doing. Usually, when they have got to know him, the ghost owners themselves accept his explanation with a just as implicit faith.

Tom, who is always true to his own gift, would go on making his statements whether they were believed or not, but it is always satisfactory to be proved right, and since I wrote this chapter I received a brief letter from Mrs. Huddleston to tell me that she had just come into possession of a fact that goes a long way towards indicating that Tom's explanation that the ghost at Sawston was a night-watchman, probably called "something like Cutlass", was absolutely correct. She wrote: "Since your visit, in fact only yesterday, we have found out that there is a family in the village called 'Cutriss'. This is quite extraordinary, as we had never heard of it, and it could so easily be the name that Mr. Corbett was hearing."

SIX

Camfield Place and Buriton Manor

TOM CORBETT is an ardent animal lover. His home, just off Sloane Square, is overrun by two dogs and at least three cats. The ill-treatment of animals is one of the few subjects that will make him very angry. He maintains that not only are animals intelligent, they are also tuned in better to psychic vibrations than human beings. He has seen his own boxer bitch, Biddy, back away, with her hackles up, from the unseen influence of a haunted room.

He has always said that animals—dogs especially—have as much right to haunt as men and women, and do. "They are individuals, aren't they?" he asks, "So they can become ghosts—although it's very rare for them to do so."

There are records of animal ghosts in Britain—usually horses which seem to do a lot of galloping around with headless riders on their backs. But probably the most valuable account of an animal haunting came, again, from Robert Graves. It is, again, contained in his autobiography *Good-bye to All That*. This incident occurred when he was on leave from France during the 1914-18 War:

"Nancy's (his wife's) brother, Tony, had also gone to France by now, and her mother made herself ill by worrying about him. Early in June he should be due to leave. I was on leave myself at the end of one of the four months' cadet courses, staying with the rest of Nancy's family at

97

Maesyneuardd, a big Tudor house near Harlech. This was the most haunted house that I have ever been in, though the ghosts, with one exception, were not visible, except occasionally in the mirrors.

"They would open and shut doors, rap on the oak panels, knock the shades off lamps, and drink the wine from the glasses at our elbows when we were not looking. The house belonged to an officer in the Second Battalion, whose ancestors had most of them died of drink.

"The visible ghost was a little yellow dog that would appear on the lawn in the early morning to announce deaths. Nancy saw it through the window that time.

"The first Spanish influenza epidemic began, and Nancy's mother caught it, but did not want to miss Tony's leave and going to the London theatres with him. So when the doctor came, she took quantities of aspirin, reduced her temperature, and pretended to be all right. But she knew that the ghosts in the mirrors knew the truth.

"She died in London on July 13th, a few days later. Her chief solace, as she lay dying, was that Tony had got his leave prolonged on her account . . . Tony was killed in September."

When Tom Corbett heard that Barbara Cartland, the romantic novelist and mother of Lady Lewisham, was haunted by the spirit of a dog, nothing could stop him making arrangements to visit her house right away. Miss Cartland's belief in the supernatural being quite as strong as his own, she said she would be delighted to receive him at Camfield Place, her home at Essendon, in Hertfordshire.

The Camfield Place estate has been in existence since the fifteenth century. But in 1867, the lovely Tudor house that stood on a hill, overlooking its 500 acres, was pulled down by an unimaginative Victorian, and a comfortable rambling, but much less picturesque mansion was built in its place.

Probably its greatest claim to fame is that Beatrix Potter, creator of the immortal Peter Rabbit, spent most of her life there. In fact, *The Tale of Peter Rabbit*, which has delighted generations of children, was conceived and written in and around the potting shed of Camfield's lovely garden. Indeed, the unimaginative Victorian was Miss Potter's grandfather.

From the vantage point of the house you can overlook a valley and the rise beyond it, along which there is an all-but invisible road where, it is claimed, the young Elizabeth I used to ride during her days at Hatfield House, not far away.

In 1950 Barbara Cartland, in real life Mrs. Hugh McCorquodale, moved in with her husband, her two sons and her dogs—like Tom Corbett, Miss Cartland never really feels at home unless there are at least two dogs at her heels.

Before she actually took possession of the house, Miss Cartland followed the policy she has pursued at the other houses she has lived in, of having Camfield Place blessed by a priest. "We always do that," she told me. "I find it often saves a lot of trouble from ghosts."

In the case of Camfield Place, there was just cause. Beatrix Potter has said that when she was very young and was sitting one evening in the huge lounge there, which was lit by twelve candles, she suddenly felt cold. Then, for no apparent reason, the candles began to go out, one after the other, as if an unseen hand was snuffing out the flames.

However, whatever it was has either faded away or was sent out of the house by the priest's blessing, for nothing quite as eerie as that has troubled the McCorquodale family since they came. Their ghost is much more mundane.

Miss Cartland's belief in the supernatural stems from when she was a young girl and went on a holiday to Carinthia with her elder brother, Ronald. While they were there they saw what was undoubtedly a ghost building—the first time I, for one, had ever heard of such a phenomenon.

"We went for a walk one day through that lovely, lonely countryside," said Miss Cartland, "and found ourselves walking beside a big lake. On the opposite bank we both saw, quite clearly, one of those magnificent, story-book castles complete with spires and turrets that seem to abound in that part of the world. When we got back to the village where we were staying we described it and the lake, and asked whom it belonged to.

"The villagers looked at us in amazement and told us that the castle had been destroyed many, many years before and was a complete ruin. They said that what remained of it didn't stand higher than six foot in any part."

It was Barbara who urged her mother, Mrs. Polly Cartland, to consult the famous medium, Estelle Roberts, during the black days of 1940 when the British Expeditionary Force had been overrun in France. Among the many who were reported missing at that time were Mrs. Cartland's two sons, Ronald and Tony. After an agonising wait the news came through that Ronald had been killed on May 30, twenty miles from Cassel. But by the summer of 1941 there was still no news of Tony. Mrs. Cartland allowed herself to be pursuaded to see Estelle Roberts at her home in Esher.

Estelle told Mrs. Cartland that both her sons were dead, and that she was in touch with them both. "The youngest one tells me he was killed the day before his brother," she said.

But Mrs. Cartland, who had made herself believe that Tony was a prisoner, refused to listen and left. On February 7, 1942, two years after he was reported missing, the news finally came through that Tony had been killed fighting a rearguard action north of Ypres on May 29, 1940—the day before Ronald's death.

"So you see," said Miss Cartland, "I am thoroughly convinced about spiritual and supernatural matters. If there was anything virulent about this house it went with the blessing. The ghosts we have now has moved in since we came. It happened this way.

"My younger son, Glen, used to have a brown and white cocker spaniel whom he adored, although it was rather acrimonious, called Jimmy. Something went wrong with the glands around Jimmy's throat and in 1955 we had to have him put down.

"I always have my doggies put to sleep here in the hall while I sit with them, so that they won't be so afraid—and that is what happened to Jimmy.

"Well, soon after that I began to notice something wrong with the other dogs at feeding time. Our dogs always feed with us in the dining-room. Their food is put down for them on either side of the double doors. We noticed that they became jumpy when they were eating and would eye something that wasn't there and bark and growl at it.

"Murray, our black and white spaniel, was particularly jumpy. He began to back away from the food as if something was threatening him. Sometimes he would jump into the air and scream as if he was being attacked.

"Then, quite recently, we have begun to see Jimmy around the place. Only the other day I went into the hall where he was put to sleep, carrying flowers in my arms.

"As I went up to the hall table to arrange them in a vase, I saw that a dog was lying under it. It registered on my mind that the dog was brown and white, but I didn't realise it until later. I thought it was Murray and put out my foot to nudge him out of the way.

"I was amazed to find that my foot didn't touch anything. And when I looked down—there was nothing there, not a dog to be seen. Then I realised that I had seen a brown and white dog, not black and white like Murray is, and that it must have been Jimmy."

Miss Cartland's maid, Miss Rose Purcell, has also seen Jimmy who, during his lifetime, was an old friend of hers whom she often took on walks.

"It was about two years ago, and I was coming into the dining-room. Just inside the door, lying curled up on the floor was a brown and white dog," she said. "It was where Jimmy always used to lie in the wintertime, and it seemed so natural that I hardly thought anything of it, and picked up my foot to step over him. Then I realised, and looked down—but he had disappeared."

Since then the harrying of the other dogs at mealtimes has grown worse. "It's becoming a bore," said Miss Cartland. "Our meals are interrupted by the squeals of pain from the dogs, and sudden jumps as they battle with this ghost for their food.

"Only the other evening, when we had people in for supper, we were continually disturbed by the growls and one-sided fights. Murray is getting more and more scared by it."

For once in his life, Tom Corbett was at a loss. He was perfectly prepared to believe that the dog's ghost was haunting Camfield Place. But he was totally unable to tune into it, to his great disappointment.

Having come to know Tom as well as I did, I knew that

something else was on his mind, besides his inability to trace the ghost of an acrimonious spaniel.

After lunch and at the end of a delightful, if fruitless visit, Miss Cartland showed us to her Victorian door. During the thanks and good-byes and general chitchat that took place there, she happened to mention that her younger son, Glen, was on a motoring tour of Europe.

I saw Tom's ears prick up. "Will you *please* tell him to be careful?" he asked Miss Cartland, "I think it's important."

A bewildered and worried Miss Cartland said she would and we drove away. In the car Tom Corbett said to me: "There's a car crash in the offing for that family. A young man is involved. I hope they'll be all right and that she warns her son."

It wasn't until a few weeks later that I heard from Miss Cartland what had happened.

Her belief that clairvoyants can get glimpses of the future, combined with her belief in Tom Corbett as a trustworthy clairvoyant, made her extremely worried. Barbara Cartland fought with her doubts for an hour or two after we had left, and then put through a phone call to Glen McCorquodale in Brussels. When he came on the phone she begged him to take care when he was driving. He promised that he would.

While she was phoning, the McCorquodale's young manservant was taking the car out of the Camfield Place garage to run down to Essendon, the nearby village.

On his way back he was involved in a crash and ended up with the car in a ditch. He escaped unhurt. The car was a complete write-off.

·   ·   ·   ·   ·

Since Camfield Place is a private house, it is not inappropriate to include in the same chapter an account of the only other visit we made to a private house. This is Buriton Manor, at Buriton, the first (or last) village in Hampshire from the Sussex border, nestling under the Downs. The name of the village is pronounced as it is often spelled, Beriton. But in the Domesday Book it figures under the name of Mapledresham. The original manor was given to Queen Matilda by William the Conqueror, but that is long gone and in its place stands a quiet, warm brick house with a plain Georgian face surrounded by green lawn.

In 1719, it was bought by the grandfather of Edward Gibbon, the historian. The great man himself lived there, although he didn't make its acquaintance until after his first term at Oxford, in 1752. Later he was to spend most of his summers at Buriton and although no part of the *Decline and Fall of the Roman Empire* was actually written at the Manor, a great deal of his preparatory reading was done here.

However, its great interest for Tom Corbett and myself arose from articles that appeared in nearly all the English national daily papers in 1957 which said that the then owner, Lt.-Col. Algernon Bonham Carter, had applied to Petersfield Rural District Council, his local authority, for a reduction in the rates he had to pay on the house *because the manor was haunted*. What is more, according to the newspaper reports of that time, the council had accepted his plea and reduced the rates accordingly by £13 a year.

If this was, in fact, correct, it showed the Rural District Council in a light that was both unusual and charming for a local authority. But although I have made inquiries, the Petersfield R.D.C. displays a curious reluctance to reveal the details of the meeting that reduced the Manor's rates, and I am very little wiser about the whole business now than I was when I began.

However, the young people who took over the house after the death of Lt.-Col. Bonham Carter, Mr. and Mrs. Miller-Sterling, said that as far as they knew the newspapers were correct and that the Manor's rates were reduced on the grounds that a ghost deducted from its value.

"There is no doubt," Mr. Miller-Sterling told us when we went to see him, "that Lt.-Col. Bonham Carter was very psychic and that the house was extremely haunted during his time." He and his wife led us out of their low-ceilinged lounge to the Georgian front door to show us the huge, graceful tithe barn which stands across the lawn facing the house. "The tradition goes that a woman servant, a chambermaid, hanged herself in that barn many, many years ago. Apparently you could hear her going out of the house across to the barn, as she did that last time in her life. I believe that the Colonel saw her more than once."

We went back into the house again. "There is an underground passage that used to lead to the church, which is just outside the grounds and which was still the chapel belonging to the manor until 1886. The Colonel's butler used to say that he could often hear footsteps walking along the passage towards the church."

Either the Miller-Sterlings are not psychic, or the ghosts that so disturbed Lt.-Col. Bonham Carter have gone, and the house once more stands quiet amid the beautiful Hampshire countryside. But a ripple of the past ran through it some years ago when their five-year-old son complained that "someone keeps trying to take my pillow away at night when I'm in bed".

The boy slept in a small, uneven-floored bedroom in the oldest part of the house. Guests who have been put there when the other eleven bedrooms in the house are full, have complained to Mr. and Mrs. Miller-Sterling that their sleep was disturbed by weird dreams. So, naturally enough, they asked Tom Corbett if he would have a look at it.

The room opens off a little passageway and overlooks the tree-shaded lawn at the back of the house. Tom stood in the centre of it for a moment or two, and then went out into and down the passage until he stopped outside a room on the left.

"The ghost goes into your son's room," he told Mrs. Miller-Sterling, "and comes down this passage to this room. It is quite distinct. It is an elderly, somehow warm-natured woman. She has the appearance of a nanny to me. She doesn't try to take away your son's pillow, she's soothing it to make him more comfortable. There's nothing to worry about. She wouldn't hurt him."

There was no connection between this comfortable person and the suicide, Tom told us—to the relief of Mr. and Mrs. Miller-Sterling.

In fact, it was the only ghost Tom could find in the whole house. He could not pick up the traces of the hanged maid, nor hear the footsteps trudging along the secret passage to the church.

However, there is some confusion about the ghost that Lt.-Col. Bonham Carter saw. The Miller-Sterlings say it was the hanged maid. But when I rang up the Colonel's brother, Admiral Sir Stuart Bonham Carter, who lived in the nearby town of Petersfield, he told me that the ghost at Buriton Manor had been a "dear little old lady", which does not sound very much like the apparition of a maid about to commit suicide. In fact, it sounds a great deal more like the "comforting nanny" that Tom Corbett described.

Tom's particular gifts have thrown him into a profession where it is almost impossible to be proved right beyond doubt. It is to his eternal credit that throughout all the visits we made, any new evidence that turned up, and about which he could not possibly have known, consistently dovetailed in with his stated findings. Although I never doubted him, I have never got over being surprised at each new display of his incredible insight. In the case of Buriton Manor, the evidence was too nebulous to prove anything to anybody. However, coming as it did, directly after our experience at Camfield Place when he saw a young man connected with the household involved in a car crash some six hours *before* it happened, I have absolutely no doubt that a nanny is haunting Buriton Manor, taking care of the children, as she did in life, and as Tom Corbett says she is.

SEVEN

Penfound Manor

✽   ✽

IN THE SPRING of 1957, a London bank manager and his wife, Mr. and Mrs. Kenneth Tucker, went to Palma, in Majorca, for a much-needed holiday.

While they were there they made friends with a middle-aged woman, also on holiday, who fancied herself as a palmist fortune teller. Now Mr. and Mrs. Tucker did not believe in the supernatural—the life of a bank manager moves strictly within the three dimensions and does not admit of a fourth.

However, to please the woman and for fun, Mr. Tucker allowed her to read his palm. She told him very definitely that in the immediate future his whole life would be changed, that he would give up his job and move to a different part of the country.

Mr. and Mrs. Tucker smiled at each other. Mr. Tucker had been with his bank for thirty-eight years, he had only a few more years to go before he retired with a respectable pension. It would take a lot, they knew, to make them give it up. "Nothing could have been more certain than that she was wrong," says Mr. Tucker.

But in October of that same year, Mr. Tucker, who suffered badly from bronchitis, had another, serious attack. The doctors told him that his only choice was to give up his job and move into the country. "Your best bet is the north Cornish coast," they said.

Bewildered and distressed at having to start a new life, the Tuckers began to search for a desirable residence in north Cornwall. It wasn't easy. They looked over house after house, liking none of them. The last house on the list the estate agent had given them, was called Penfound Manor. Without any great hope, the Tuckers drove out to look at it.

At Poundstock the nearest village to the manor, they stopped to ask directions, and, having got them, drove on.

As they went they began to find themselves driving through a bewildering maze of quiet lanes which make an ornate pattern through the steep rocky fields of that part. The further they went the less they could see. They were driving through what were almost passages between banks and hedges that had been built and trained to stand ten foot high. They might have been the only people in Cornwall. Only the seagulls overhead and the salt in the air told them they were nearing the Atlantic.

They sensed that they were in old smuggling country and that the banks and hedges had been carefully prepared to shield the sight of covered wagons with their illicit cargo from the exciseman's gaze.

They passed and re-passed the entrance to the Manor four times without knowing it. Penfound is the best-hidden home in England. Finally, in desperation, they stopped at the only human habitation in sight, an old grey farmhouse. They were directed down the unpropitious-looking track that turned off the lane beside the farmhouse. At the bottom of this they turned left and stopped.

Penfound Manor is surrounded on all sides by an old wall. Inlet into it is a wrought iron tracery gate. The Tuckers went through it and into a courtyard. Trees enfolded it, a fountain rose from the flagstones and the flowers swayed in the salt-tanged breeze.

In front of them, seeming to grow out of the flags, was the loveliest old house they had ever seen. It was low and rambling. Diamond-pane glass winked out between the fronds of red creeper. The roof was uneven with age and moss grew between tiny slates.

"It was like coming across a lovely secret," said Mr. Tucker. "As we walked through the old gate I was reaching for my cheque book. I don't think either of us slept or ate until the place was ours.

"We realised from the first that this was a place we should share. So in the following year we opened it to the public. We didn't expect more than six or ten people because it is so unknown and remote. We got 2,000. The following year about 10,000 visitors came. There is something about Penfound that gets hold of people."

Whatever it was, it also wound itself tightly round the Tuckers who long devoted themselves with almost fanatical enthusiasm to delving into the history of their home, searching among old manuscripts and records until they built up a remarkably comprehensive picture of the Penfounds of Penfound.

Their most curious discovery, however, was that the date of April 26 has a frightening significance for the local people. "We couldn't understand at first," said Mr. Tucker, "why, on that day every year, nobody would come near the place. One year, late on April 26 we had a burst pipe, but nothing we could do would get anyone up here to mend it until the following day. There were other incidents like that. Something seemed to scare them off on that date.

"Mind you, there was no admission that they were scared. They always had some reasonable excuse—they were decorating, or attending their grandmother's funeral or something.

"Gradually we have found out that a ghost is supposed

to walk at Penfound on that day. They say it is the ghost of a young and pretty girl, Kate Penfound, who lived here in the seventeenth century."

Bit by bit the Tuckers pieced together the sad legend of Kate Penfound and the reason for her haunting. They had never seen her on April 26, or any other day for that matter, so their scepticism remained intact, although Tom Corbett and I thought when we met them that it was beginning to show cracks. Both referred to her as if she were a living person and, as Mrs. Tucker said, "Some very funny things have happened."

.   .   .   .   .

The original Penfound, which has been incorporated into the house, was a huge single room, now the Great Hall, and belonged to Queen Edith, wife of Edward the Confessor. Excavations have found that beneath the present floor of the Great Hall is another of trampled-down sheep's knuckles, dating back to that period.

"The present floor is only 300 years old," said Mr. Tucker. "So in comparison, it's hardly settled down yet."

After the Norman Conquest, William gave the manor to his half brother, Robert, the Count of Mortain, although a Saxon called Briend, who had rented it from Queen Edith, was allowed to continue his tenancy. The entry in the Domesday Book reads: "Briend holds Penfou of the Count of Mortain. . . . There is one plough with one serf and two bordars, and two acres of meadow, and ten acres of pasture. In time past it was worth twenty shillings, and so now."

And that was the last time that "Penfou"—the name means head of a stream—was owned by anyone with claims to nobility. Soon after, the family who took their name from their home, moved in. They may even have been descendants of Briend the Saxon. None of the Penfounds so much as received a Knighthood, though they reigned supreme there from this time to the Jacobite Rebellion.

Mr. Tucker, who had come to know them and love them, described them as "stubborn, thrifty, quarrelsome, land-hungry, shrewd, and hard-working men with pride in their homes and their ancestry. Good friends, dangerous enemies, arrogant and high-handed, but merry and straightforward even in villainy."

Above all else they were loyal. They remained royalists down to the last man and woman through the centuries. They became ruined due to their participation on the King's side during the Civil War and eventually lost their beloved home through their support of the Jacobite Rebellion in 1745. The last of the direct line died in Poundstock's poorhouse in 1847.

However, in their hey-day the Penfounds counted in Cornwall, and each generation, out of their prosperity, beautified and added to the barn-like home of Briend the Saxon.

The first addition was a Norman wing, built by a go-ahead Penfound on to the south-west corner of the Great Hall. It incorporated three distinctly new ideas for those days. In the first place it was a Ladies' Bower, and privacy for the woman was a revolutionary thought. Secondly, it had a second storey, another new-fangled notion with, most modern of all, a private bedroom called the Solar. It remained the only bedroom at Penfound for 400 years.

During the reign of King John, the Penfounds took another step towards civilisation and built a chimney into the Great Hall. Usually in those days the house was guarded from any evil which might enter it through the chimney by a bullock's heart hung on a string. The Penfounds had an even surer charm, however—a bottle of Holy Water from the blessed River Jordan brought home by a crusading Penfound. It was said that the blessing over the river stopped the water from evaporating. Nobody has dared to find out if there is any left in the bottle up the Penfound chimney, however, since there is a curse that says whoever removes it will have the chimney fall on his head, and the Tuckers have decided to leave well alone.

In December, 1356, a tragedy took place at Poundstock's village church, leaving it haunted ever since. The victim was one of the Penfounds, clerk of the church, who was celebrating mass. Bishop Grandisson, of Exeter, in his register for 1357 gives an account of what happened:

"Certain satellites of Satan, names unknown, on the Feast of St. John the Apostle—which makes the crime worse—broke into the Parish Church of Poundstock within our Diocese with a host of armed men during Mass, and before Mass was scarcely completed they furiously entered the Chancel and with swords and staves cut down William Penfoun, clerk.

"Vestments and other Church ornaments were desecrated with human blood in contempt of the Creator, in contempt of the Church, to the subversion of ecclesiastical liberty and the disturbance of the peace of the realm. Where will we be safe from crime if the Holy Church, our Mother, the House of God and the Gateway to Heaven, is thus deprived of its sanctity?"

There is no record of what had aroused the wrath of the "satellites of Satan", but it must be remembered that, if Chaucer is to be believed, the clerks of those days were not as holy as they should have been, and not above fraternising a little too closely with other men's wives.

Whatever their reason, the two ringleaders of the assassins, John Bevill, and Simon de St. Gennys, who had been quickly arrested, were both pardoned at their trial. And poor William Penfoun has been seen wandering unrevenged, around his church ever since.

The Penfounds appear a lot in the old records of the Duchy after this. Sometimes they are on the side of the law acting as justices of the peace. December 13, 1472: "Commission of John Penfoun (and others) to inquire into the complaint of Martyn Perys, master of the ship *Le Katerine*, of Castro in Spain, and Peter Sauns, merchant and owner of the goods and merchandise in the said ship, that when the said ship was sailing at sea laden with 82 tons and one pipe of white wine of Rochelle and other goods to the value of £536 certain pirates in a ship called *La Barbara* of Fowey (John Barkeley, master), came upon them and despoiled them of the ship, wines, goods and merchandise, contrary to the form of the truce between the King (Edward IV) and his kinsman the King of Spain, and to cause restitution to be made."

Sometimes it was they who were being accused.

1553: "Petition to Sir Thomas Audeley, Lord Chancellor, by Morys Donne and his wife Julyan, widow of John Trenger, that John Trenger has held 300 acres of pasture, 300 acres of land, 100 acres of meadow, 40 acres of wood, and 600 acres of furze and heath in Cornwall, which he gave in trust to Sir John Chamonde and others for his wife Julyan after his death, but Thomas, William and Edmund Penfounde have wrongfully seized and refused to surrender them."

There is little doubt that Arthur Penfound, who made the Stuart additions and alterations to the ever-growing, ever-beautiful Manor between 1635 and 1645, was a smuggler of no small degree. It may even have been he who commanded that the hedges and banks around his home should be raised so high. Certainly, during his time valuable cargo was secretly run from Millock Bay, up the old west road to Penfound, and his remaining descendants say that he killed an exciseman who had been getting in his way.

It is at this point, in 1649, when the Royalist forces were at last subdued, that the Poundstock church records abruptly stop. It was not unusual for Royalists of that time to destroy church records so that they would not provide information for the hated Roundheads. Presumably this is what happened in the case of Poundstock, because they start again eleven years afterwards, at the end of the Commonwealth.

Nevertheless, it is a great pity, because if Kate Penfound, who is now supposed to haunt the manor, lived at all and died at all, her death would have been registered among those missing records. If, as the story goes, she was old enough to be romantically involved in the feuding Royalist and Roundhead factions she must have been born before 1649 and died during the Cromwellian rule. However, much as he had tried to find some evidence of her existence, Mr. Tucker was never able to uncover a record of her birth, or her death.

But where the records fail, legend has taken over, and from that we get a surprisingly vivid picture of Kate Penfound. You can see her with her dainty lace collar round her shoulders, running in and out between the shadow of the cool dairy and the sunlit courtyard, or helping to lead her father's horses along the cobbled path that ran straight through the house to the watering trough by the well at the back. That well, incidentally, has been the only water supply to Penfound for 900 years—and still is.

Most clearly of all you can see her in her neat, white-washed bedroom—the former Norman solar—looking out over the lovely courtyard, a dreamy, high-spirited, self-willed adolescent girl in love for the first time.

Legend doesn't say who her father was, but Mr. Tucker had worked it out that the only person it could have been was the smuggling Arthur Penfound. That fits the facts as far as it goes because legend *does* say that Kate's father was an ardent royalist—a description that fits Arthur like a glove. His own father had fought with the King's General in the West, Sir Richard Grenville, in the Civil War, and was killed at Stratton in 1643.

This is the Penfound Legend: It was Kate's misfortune that she had fallen in love with the young John Trebarfoot, the son of their close neighbours at Trebarfoot Manor three miles away. If it hadn't been for the war, Arthur might have been well pleased to match his daughter with a Trebarfoot. One of Kate's ancestors had married a John Trebarfoot in 1598, presumably with general rejoicing.

But the war had turned brother against brother and neighbour against neighbour and the Trebarfoots had declared for Cromwell, making themselves loathsome traitors in Penfound eyes. The only recourse for the two lovers in this situation was to elope.

So, the story goes, on the night of April 26—year unknown—young Kate hitched up her skirts and climbed out of the solar window to the courtyard below where John Trebarfoot was waiting for her. But her father discovered them before they were able to slip away; and here the legend divides: some people say that he shot them both as they stood locked in each others arms in the porch. Others, that he and the Trebarfoot drew their swords and fought a duel. Kate was killed trying to separate them and then the two men fought to a finish, killing each other.

Since records show that Arthur Penfound died quietly at

Winkleigh in Devon in 1656, the former is the more acceptable version.

As I say, Mr. Tucker had been unable to find any evidence at all to corroborate the life and death of this Civil War Juliet. But he was puzzled by the persistence of the legend locally.

"They still refer to her," he said. "She is very real to the people around here. And the legend, although it is so vague about dates, is very exact in its details. It even pinpoints the hollow oak tree outside the main gates as the place where the lovers used to leave their letters for one another. Then there is this tenacious belief that Penfound is haunted. When we first moved in, everybody kept asking us, 'Have you seen Kate lately?' They gave details of her ghost, which, they said, would materialise in her room, walk down the Stuart staircase, through the bower across the Great Hall and up the main staircase and then disappear. All this and their avoidance of the house on April 26 puzzles us quite a lot. But we have found Kate so attractive that we have included her and her legend in our tour of the house for visitors."

Even more puzzling to the sceptical Mr. and Mrs. Tucker were the odd reactions of some of their psychic visitors.

Mrs. Tucker was showing a party of tourists round the house during the first year the house was opened to the public, and, having reached Kate's bedroom, was telling them the legend when she noticed a man and his wife exchange an odd glance. "It seems my wife is psychic," the man told her afterwards. "When we came to the gate to enter the courtyard, she said, 'Oh, I can't go in here. Something dreadful happened here.' It took all my persuasion to stop her turning round and going home."

More recently, Mr. Tucker was in charge of a party

which included a very stout woman. "We had done the ground floor," said Mr. Tucker, "and we had reached the little Stuart staircase which leads up to Kate's room when the stout lady asked if I would mind her remaining downstairs in the Great Hall. Her weight was too much, she said, to drag up that staircase. Now she didn't know anything about the Kate legend from me, because we don't tell it to our visitors until we are actually upstairs in her bedroom.

"When we came downstairs the woman was missing. I went to look for her and found her sitting in the porch, looking a little upset. I asked her if she was all right. She said: 'I couldn't remain in there. It's haunted. I'm a medium, you see, and suddenly I had the most terrible pain in my stomach as if someone had stabbed me.'

"I was getting a bit impatient with her, thinking she was putting it on, then she said, 'And another thing, a name kept going through my mind. Did anyone ever live here called something like Editha?'

"Well, that stopped me a bit in my tracks, because, of course, the house did once belong to Queen Edith, although I didn't see how the woman knew that. What's more, in the Domesday Book the Queen is referred to as Eddeva."

As we heard out Mr. and Mrs. Tucker's tale, Tom Corbett and I were sitting with them in Edith's Great Hall, with the sun dappling scarlet and blue around us as it filtered through the window, made of glass from Westminster Abbey.

Tom shook his head and said, "Murder leaves something behind—an atmosphere, an influence that can never quite be wiped away. I can't feel anything of that in this house, and your courtyard is a happy place."

We went up the winding Stuart staircase to Kate's bedroom, with its whitewashed walls, old rose carpet and four-poster bed. Tom liked it, but again he could find no trace of sudden death.

"There is a slight entity here," he said. "Almost just a memory of a woman, pleasant, young—a definite character. There is nothing unhappy about this room, and there would have been if she had been killed as the legend says she was. Either the legend is wrong or this is not the bedroom."

But although he visited nearly every room in the house, spending some time in each, Tom was unable to find one trace of a ghost. He did suggest to Mr. Tucker that excavations at the back of the house, where there stands an ancient wall, might be fruitful from the archaeological viewpoint. "But there are no ghosts that I can find," he said.

I don't know whether Mr. and Mrs. Tucker were disappointed or relieved, at Tom's inability to uncover their ghost. Some years of living with the idea that their house was haunted had made them almost accustomed to it.

Then, again, there had been very reliable second-hand reports from the descendants of people who saw her during the early years of this century. "The house used to be looked after by a Mr. Stacey, who was the hind or bailiff for the then owner," said Mr. Tucker. "One day last year Mr. Stacey's son, a well-educated city man, came round on a tour of the house with a party and introduced himself.

"As he had known the house, we compared notes. And in the course of the conversation he asked me if my wife and I had seen any 'manifestations' as he called them. I said 'Good heavens, no'. And he told us that his father, who had been a very level-headed man, had seen the ghost several times. He left it at that."

But not long afterwards when Mr. Tucker was showing another party round the house, a couple came up to him and the wife said: 'I never thought you would tell the story of Kate. Hasn't she frightened you yet?'

"It appears that the wife's father used to work for Mr. Stacey and he and his family lived in a cottage near the house.

"One night he came here to the Manor to talk over some business with Mr. Stacey. They sat there in the Great Hall in front of the fire chatting when all of a sudden the father saw a woman come out of the bower and cross the Great Hall heading for the main stairs. He knew from her clothes and her ghostly appearance that it was Kate. He pointed her out with a shaking finger to Mr. Stacey, but Mr. Stacey didn't seem at all disturbed. 'Oh we get quite used to her,' he said. 'We never take any notice now.' But the father got up, ran out of the house and all the way home. His daughter said she remembers him arriving, white and obviously shaken. She said the compelling thing about his story was that although he told it many, many times during the rest of his life, not one detail of it ever varied.

"And since we have been in occupation, we have received many letters from past owners telling about the strange things that happened here."

But despite this quite unusual weight of evidence, Tom refused to change his opinion and declare the house haunted. He has never pandered to legend unless his fourth dimensional vision has told him it is based on fact, and for all Penfound's charm, he wasn't going to start now.

If ghosts fade away in time—and Tom is sure that they do, it may be that Kate, too, has disappeared from the scene.

On the way out, Mr. Tucker pointed out to us, near the

The author with Tom Corbett and Lord Montagu at Beaulieu

His Grace The Duke of Bedford and Tom Corbett in the haunted
bedroom at Woburn Abbey

tracery gate, a sundial which marks the spot where a Judas tree was planted by Thomas Penfound, Arthur's son and therefore probably Kate's brother, to mark the family's horror at the execution of Charles I on January 30, 1649. For many years it was believed locally that the tree would flourish until Thomas Penfound, fervent royalist that he was, became reconciled to Oliver Cromwell in heaven.

It stood for 270 years. Then, one day in 1920, a strange thing happened, according to records of that time. A single, solitary cloud appeared in a perfectly clear sky and moved until it was stationed over Penfound Manor. There was no rain, but suddenly out of the cloud came a shaft of lightning which scorched and withered the Judas tree. Perhaps Kate was involved in the general reconciliation and stopped haunting—for no eye-witness reports of her ghost have been given since that date.

Whatever happened, we walked out of Penfound's tracery gate leaving Kate Penfound as much of an enigma as she always was. And perhaps, in an age when too much is docketed and clarified, an enigma now and then isn't a bad thing.

EIGHT

West Wycombe Park

ONE HOT summer's night in or around 1753, a group of men grotesquely dressed in white parodies of monks' habits gathered in the carefully-ruined chapel of Medmenham Abbey by the side of the Thames. Outside the moonlight fell on statues and urns meticulously arranged around the grounds to cast shadows of Gothic gloom. Inside, lamps lit up pictures, decorations and an altar which displayed most of the obscenities and blasphemies known to man.

The air was thick with the choking smell of sinister herbs as the twelve men went through a travesty of the communion service. The mock Abbot, in white and scarlet, blessed his flock in the name of Lucifer and led them to the refectory where, after a solemn grace, they began to drink as if their life depended on it. By the time they had sung every bawdy song in their considerable repertoire, they were ready for the women. The door was flung open, and in came a giggling gaggle of ladies dressed as nuns. Under the demure cowls and wimples were faces that were well-known in the London brothels.

The first meeting of the Friars of St. Francis had reached the high spot of its night.

Of all the notorious clubs, especially the Hell-Fire Clubs, that sprang up in England like fungi during this period of the eighteenth century, this became the most infamous—although it is doubtful if it were the worst morally. Perhaps its distinguished membership had something to do with its notoriety. As a founder, the club had a man who was soon to be the country's Chancellor of the Exchequer, Sir Francis Dashwood. At the first and subsequent meetings were enrolled men like Lord Sandwich, First Lord of the Admiralty; George Bubb Dodington, Baron of Melcombe Regis and a cabinet minister; Thomas Potter, son of the Archbishop of Canterbury, Paymaster-General and Joint Vice-Treasurer of Ireland; the Earl of March; and John Wilkes, the political writer and orator. It is said that Hogarth was another, though less frequent visitor to Medmenham revels.

The light from the black tapers in the Medmenham chapel fell on faces that were, it is true, lustful, debauched and shameless. But they were faces that were also marked, more often than not, with strong intelligence and humour. And the hands that passed the wafers of the Black communion, controlled between them the reins that governed England. They were the rakes of a socially-turbulent age that produced too many rakes and too many puritans. Most of them had exhausted the pleasures of simple wenching and now needed elaboration and ceremony. In nearly all of them this jaded palate existed side by side with an almost psychopathic wish to revile what they regarded as a hypocritical church.

The genius who provided the outlet for all this frustration and founded the Brotherhood of Medmenham was, perhaps, the most interesting character of them all.

Sir Francis Dashwood had inherited his title and his ancestral home—West Wycombe Park in Buckinghamshire—at sixteen from his father, who was something of a rake himself, having married four heiresses in his time.

Francis' name has gone down into history as an almost legendary villain and lecher, but the man was a puzzling mixture of virtue and vice—and, on the whole, the virtue outweighed the vice. He had, for instance, tremendous kindness. In an era that was riddled with political corruption, he managed to remain an honest, if not a very great politician. He possessed considerable moral courage and was a great fighter on behalf of lost causes. He did everything humanly possible to try to save the life of Admiral Byng, who was made the scapegoat for the naval failure to relieve the siege of Minorca and eventually shot.

Francis' "sin" was his over-sensuality and the fact that he had the money to indulge it. He had adolescent fantasies, that he never grew out of, which made him adore dressing up. By the time he was forty he had racketed around the Continent to his heart's content, tasting every pleasure it had to offer. But by the time he returned to England to settle down he was no more mature than he had been when he was twenty.

He had already become a faithful and enthusiastic member of some exotic clubs, but they did not really meet his more lusty requirements. Vague plans for the perfect club that would provide its members with excitement, women and blasphemy took shape in his head. Then he met Francis Duffield, a young landowner whose ancient home, Medmenham Abbey, was about six miles away from West Wycombe Park. It had been a Cistercian monastery for many centuries before the Reformation and an odour of sanctity still pervaded it. It would, thought Francis, be the ideal headquarters for a desecratory club aping the old monasteries.

Some years before, Francis Dashwood's portrait had been painted depicting him as St. Francis with a halo

124

round his head, kneeling and gazing longingly at a nude Venus. The joke stuck in his mind as an excellent one and, now that he had found the ideal headquarters, he saw no reason against carrying it even further and forming around St. Francis a like-minded band of brothers. He and Duffield formed an agreement and work was put in hand to transform the Abbey and its private chapel into a shrine for Devil worshippers.

Exactly what Freudian reason was behind Dashwood's desire to derogate the church is not known. Whatever it was, it was strong and found no lack of sympathisers. It is doubtful whether any of the members believed in the occult art they practised, nevertheless the black mumbo jumbo gave them an outlet for mocking the religion they had all turned against.

Membership of the club was divided into two groups of twelve. The first twelve were the Apostles, the superior order, who were privy to the more salacious rites. The other twelve, the inferior order, were merely occasional guests and drinking companions.

The Apostles met for about a fortnight's unalloyed debauchery every summer. Exactly what went on at those meetings is not now known. The club's minute book was righteously destroyed in Edwardian days and all we are left with are some lurid glimpses, probably misleading, given to us by disapproving contemporaries. There is no doubt that after the "service" there were riotous drinking bouts which ended in each brother retiring with a woman, either to his beautifully equipped "cell" or to the shadowed grounds.

The Brotherhood remained intact and flourishing for at least ten years, probably longer, before it had to disband. A contributory factor to its tremendous success was, without doubt, the marital unhappiness of most of the members. For nearly all of them it was a relief to get away from home and mingle with women who, even if their morals were non-existent, were at least out to please. Sir Francis himself, for instance, had a wife who was described by his enemy Horace Walpole as "a poor, forlorn Presbyterian prude". Lord Sandwich's marriage with a woman twenty-two years older than himself failed disastrously. Dodington promised his mistress that he would never marry anyone else, giving her a £10,000 bond on his word, so that when he did marry he had to keep it a secret for seventeen years until the mistress died and involuntarily released him from the bond. Paul Whitehead, who was the faithful steward of the club, had married a rich, but ugly and half-witted heiress, and John Wilkes was formally separated from his ageing wife.

For such men the excellent wine and the obliging nuns of Medmenham must have provided a badly needed opiate. But it couldn't last. Gradually tales, often highly exaggerated, began to leak out about the scandals that were being carried on by famous men at the Abbey.

By 1763 the Brotherhood had begun to decay. Bubb Dodington and Potter were dead, Francis Duffield had died at the age of twenty-six and at least two others were dying of drink. The club was being openly attacked by two of its former brethren, one of whom was John Wilkes who had eventually become disgusted with it. The nation was beginning to murmur. Sir Francis realised that the days of Medmenham were over and the club was disbanded before there was further open scandal.

Francis retired to his estates above the village of West Wycombe. But he didn't give up. His youthful, enthusiastic temperament never failed him. With the equally enthusiastic and loyal Paul Whitehead he began to think up ways and means of continuing the club in a different headquarters where the remaining brothers could meet. He came across the ideal place on his own doorstep.

Many years before, when there had been serious unemployment among his villagers, Sir Francis Dashwood had provided work for them by paying for a road to be built, straight as a dye, from the town of High Wycombe to the village of West Wycombe. (Whatever the rest of the world thought of him, his own villagers were very fond of Sir Francis. He had, after all, spent £6,000 of his own money—an enormous sum then—on building them a church on the top of the hill opposite the one his own house stood on. And although it was built to his own design and is probably the least religious-looking church in the British Isles, it was at least erected by him for them).

The chalk for the road came from some prehistoric caves which had been found tunnelling into the hill opposite the West Wycombe Park gates. By the time they had been mined they had become a labyrinth of dripping corridors and high-vaulted caverns, running a quarter of a mile into the hill. Now Dashwood looked at them with new, calculating eyes and decided that their eerie gloom would provide the ideal headquarters for his Franciscans.

Paul Whitehead set up his cellar in one of the smaller caves, the others were furnished as comfortably as possible and Lord Sandwich and the remaining Friars came down from London to continue their old revels. Newcomers were introduced to the Brotherhood and local girls as well as London prostitutes were recruited to provide the entertainment.

But the old zest was going, try to hide it though they might. There was a hollow ring about the laughter and shouting that echoed round the Wycombe tunnels that was not caused by the acoustics alone. Lord Sandwich, who was being harried politically, found it difficult to forget his business troubles as he had done. Paul White-head's life of lechery had made him into a senile old man before his time, and even St. Francis' fantastic powers were beginning to fail him.

The meetings of the club gradually and imperceptibly began to fall off. Gradually Paul Whitehead established a respectable life and would spend his days taking tea with his neighbours. Within six months of each other, Mrs. Whitehead and Lady Dashwood died—and their husbands were amazed to find what grief this caused them.

In 1774, Whitehead fell sick with an illness that baffled his doctors. He sneered at them for their ignorance—he, at least, knew that it was fatal. Three months later he died. He directed that his heart should be taken out of his body after death, embalmed and given to his old friend Francis to put in a marble urn in his mausoleum. This was done with tremendous pomp and ceremony—but in 1839 some-body stole it.

After his wife's death, Francis had taken a mistress, a Mrs. Barry, by whom he had a daughter, Rachel Antonina Lee, destined to grow up into as great an eccentric as her father. Gradually, Francis was forced to retire into respectable domesticity, and one of the last pictures we have of the old rake is his mistress reading a novel to him as he sits by the fire in the evenings.

This quiet comfort was disturbed during 1781, the last year of his life, when Paul Whitehead's ghost was seen time and again, sliding between the trees and bushes of the grounds, beckoning to his old friend. Lady Austen, Francis' sister, told her friend William Cowper, the poet, that the spectre had been seen more than once by every member of the household, both by day and by night. The old Abbot was being beckoned towards death by the most faithful of his friends. There were other signs and omens, as well. A stain like five red fingers appeared on the marble tablet erected in the church to the memory of the first Sir Francis. Frightened, superstitious villagers tried to wash it off, but it refused to go.

Inevitably, Sir Francis became ill. But he refused to give up his lust for life. They laid him in bed in an upstairs room where he lay planning another trip to Italy, to revisit the scenes of his old revels. He arranged for a friend to come with him, and even had his bags packed. But by the day of his proposed departure, he was dead and his broken-hearted sister was already planning the epitaph that was to be put in the family vault: "To the Memory of Francis, Baron Le Despenser, who was Treasurer of the Chambers, Chancellor of the Exchequer, Master of the Wardrobe, and joint Postmaster-General. He departed this life Dec. 11th 1781, aged 73 years. Revered, beloved and regretted by all who knew him."

.   .   .   .   .

The caves at West Wycombe had proved a disappointment—ghostwise, that is. Tom Corbett and I had driven down Francis road from High Wycombe to West Wycombe village, climbed up the hill and plunged into the dank caves through the arch that Sir Francis had built in his beloved Gothic style two hundred years before. Our guide was his descendant and namesake, Sir Francis Dashwood, who had taken over much of the estate management from his father, the previous owner of West Wycombe Park, Sir John Dashwood, before the latter died.

We stumbled along behind him as he toured us round the corridors and caverns which he has restored as near as possible to their condition during the Franciscan Friars' days, and which are now attracting thousands of visitors every year.

However, they housed no ghosts. Tom Corbett couldn't pick up the slightest trace of a spirit. There was, he said, no reason why he should. Because someone is debauched it does not mean that they are automatically going to become ghosts and haunt the scene of their debauchery.

It was the same at the church, where Sir Francis spent so many hours in his dotage sitting quietly in the huge, golden dome that adorns its top, looking out over his lands. Tom looked over it very carefully, but could pick up no evidence that the man had ever returned to it.

But if we weren't finding his ghost, we were at least learning a lot about Sir Francis Dashwood. His namesake is a great admirer of his ancestor who, he says, is often much maligned. "He was a very generous man," he told us. "He set up a tremendous standard of philanthropy in the village." There is no doubt that the reputation the old rake most justly earned has proved something of an embarrassment to his family ever since. It gave the public the idea that all Dashwoods are lusty, rumbustious, rip-roaring heathens. In fact, the Dashwoods have been a more religious family than most. They have been Puritans for centuries, are the closest living descendants of the poet Milton and fought for Parliament during the Civil War. And they have turned out more than their fair share of clergymen and respected members of parliament.

Neither Sir John nor his son believed very strongly in ghosts, although Sir Francis admitted that he felt a strong dislike for some rooms in the house, without being able to say why. However, there have been one or two very strange incidents in the past which stopped them from becoming complete disbelievers.

In the 1930s, for instance, a guest who had lingered overlong over his port was sitting in solitary state in the dining-room when suddenly he jumped up and came rushing out, looking extremely upset. He had, he said, lifted up his eyes from his glass to look round the empty room and found that in unearthly silence he had been joined by eleven ghost figures, who were sitting round the table with him. As we know, Sir Francis had a predilection for the number twelve as far as guests went. But as Tom Corbett could find nothing in the dining-room the incident has to remain unexplained.

Then, again, around the same time, Noel Coward, who was visiting the house, and was sitting in the saloon playing the piano, found that there was someone leaning against the piano looking down at him. Coward looked up, to come face to face with an amiable, smiling monk, who then disappeared.

On another occasion, a school friend of Francis Dashwood's, staying for the holidays, saw the figure of an old monk in one of the rooms and spent the rest of his visit highly apprehensive that he might see it again.

It was a hot and lovely spring day when Tom, Sir Francis and myself drove up the hill from the entrance to the Park to the house that his ancestor built. You approach it from the west and go in through a portico decorated with six pillars, in imitation of a Greek temple to Bacchus. The east portico, in the Doric style, is a reproduction of a temple to Venus; the north side is Corinthian and on the south the house becomes a Venetian loggia. It looks exotic, and slightly out of place in the English spring countryside—however, Sir Francis did his best to alter that, too. It is said that he had his gardens laid out in the figure of a woman. But if he did, the shrubs, pillars and mounds with which he marked 'the various parts of her anatomy have long since gone.

The immensely varied temples with which Sir Francis

decorated nearly every hillock, promontory and lake island around the house, still stand, empty and decaying. However, a dash of new life has come to them since his namesake descendant has been using them to house his fancy-dress parties.

The hand of Sir Francis is as discernible inside the house as it is on the outside and in the grounds. All the rooms—and it has twenty-five bedrooms—are in sumptuous Italian style with painted ceilings, and ornate, magnificently-framed portraits hang on the walls. In one of the upstairs rooms there is a ceiling decorated with Masonic symbols, some of them inverted.

We scoured the house, the caves, the church and the gardens. The baronet even punted Tom and I over to the temple on the island in the lake, in case a ghost had decided to take up residence there. But apart from the general feeling in the atmosphere that "Sir Francis was a very much nicer man than history makes him out to be", Tom could find nothing more.

There is only one ghost at West Wycombe Park and that is of the utmost charm and respectability. Tom found it in the Music Saloon. "It's a woman," he said. "An extremely beautiful woman, and her hair is drawn softly back from her face and parted in the centre. It's greying a little. She was a great hostess in her day. She favoured the colour blue. She is a fairly recent ghost, and has only come back now because she is happy here and wants to express her approval of what is being done for the house." He turned to Sir Francis: "I feel she is recent enough for you to have known her."

"Oh," said Sir Francis, "You mean my grandmother. That fits her exactly."

Although he looked for it, Tom couldn't find, either, the ghost of Paul Whitehead which was seen so frequently two hundred years ago. Since no one ever did see it after the death of Sir Francis it seems likely that Whitehead was only waiting for his old friend's company before he turned his back on his old haunts for ever.

If our visit to West Wycombe didn't produce many ghosts, however, it did at least add to the sum of our knowledge about them in general. We knew now that the popular idea that a dissolute life leads to ghosthood beyond the grave is not necessarily right.

A man may be sinful, but may still be spiritually aware. Sir Francis was, otherwise he would not have taken so much trouble to trample spiritual matters in the dust. With all his faults he was very much the unwitting product of a bad age. I don't wish to whitewash him, but it seems to me that much may be forgiven in retrospect to a man who was, as one historian says, "the most likeable and interesting rake in the time of the Georges."

NINE

Brede

❋ ❋

ALL I KNEW about Brede Place, in Sussex, before I arrived there on a misty afternoon one autumn were a few basic details and an anecdote I had learned from Mr. Goldsmith at Salisbury Hall.

It was a Churchill story he had given me to add to a lifetime's collection of Churchill stories:

"Clare Frewen, who later became Clare Sheridan, the sculptress, was a frequent visitor to Salisbury Hall at one time. She used to come to see her aunt, Lady Randolph Churchill and her cousin, Winston. At her marriage to Wilfred Sheridan, Winston asked her how she was going to spend her honeymoon.

" 'We are going to Brede,' said Clare. 'I suspected that,' said Churchill, 'where are you going to stay?' "

It is an easy trap to fall into—Brede Place always being referred to as just Brede.

In fact, on the way down to visit the house I found myself lost at the nearby village of Northiam, and sticking my head out of the car window I had asked the police constable on duty there, "Can you tell me the way to Brede?" before I stopped to think.

But either the constable lacked Churchillian opportunism or had got tired of the joke. He just said: "Turn left, miss. . . ."

It would, I reflected as I drove on, have been simpler all round if the property had retained its original name of Bretda, which is what it was called in the time of Queen Emma, wife of Ethelred the Unready and, later, King Canute.

Add to these snippets the knowledge that the house was very haunted, and that was the sum of my information about Brede as I parked outside its massive stone walls and went in—to find that Tom Corbett had already arrived. But I didn't remain in ignorance for long. When we met them, Mr. and Mrs. Moreton Frewen had lived at Brede with their four children for about ten years. They had, moreover, got the history of the house at their finger-tips and had already collected a miniature library dealing with its hauntings.

Brede was an outpost of France on what was then the Sussex coast, long before William the Conqueror invaded England. In 1017 the French-born Emma had persuaded her second husband, Canute, to make it over to the Abbey of Fécamp in Normandy. So, when William landed at Hastings eight miles away forty-nine years later, he already had a foot, as it were, in the Saxon camp. It probably influenced his choice of landing place. It was one of the few places he spared when he laid waste the south coast in his progress towards London and the throne.

About 1350, the land was acquired by a Sir Thomas atte Ford and he built on it the earliest example of an unfortified manor in southern England. In 1395 it passed by marriage to the Oxenbridge family, who held it for over two hundred years. With a few Elizabethan alterations it is still essentially the same house today. In 1708 it became part of the Frewen estates, an adjunct to their main house at Northiam.

It was about this time that the Brede villagers began to

call the manor house "haunted" and to give it a wide berth
—a wariness that exists among some of them even now.

No doubt it was haunted then, but the more fantastic
stories about it—that it was roamed at night by a giant
Oxenbridge, who ate babies—were carefully nurtured, and
probably thought up, by a bunch of smugglers who were
hand in glove with the tenant of that time and who wanted
no witnesses to their illegal traffic.

In 1895 Mr. and Mrs. Moreton Frewen moved in to do
the house up before letting it out to Stephen Crane, the
American writer. For the Christmas of 1899, Stephen
Crane put on a private pantomime at Brede. It was called
The Ghost and dealt with the smugglers' legend of the
baby-eating giant. No pantomime can ever have had such
distinguished collaboration. Crane called in all his literary
friends and visitors to Brede and made each of them contribute at least a line to the script.

When it was finally performed, the programme read,
The Ghost, by Mr. Henry James, Mr. Robert Barr, Mr.
George Gissing, Mr. Rider Haggard, Mr. Joseph Conrad,
Mr. H. B. Marriott-Watson, Mr. H. G. Wells, Mr. Edwin
Pugh, Mr. A. E. W. Mason and Mr. Stephen Crane. Mr.
Mason played the part of the ghost and Mrs. H. G. Wells
provided background music on the piano.

Apart from smugglers' tales, however, there are authen-
ticated reports of hauntings at Brede, and here Mr. Frewen
broke off his history and turned to Tom Corbett.

"Would you like to look round before I tell you any
more, so that you can form your own conclusions?" he
asked.

Tom said he would very much, and we all moved away
from the great hall with its huge Tudor fireplace to tour
the house.

The operative adjective for Brede is medieval. The

Elizabethans made a smaller impression on this house than any other I have seen. True, they put a ceiling on the Great Hall which used to reach up to the rafters. They built chimneys and closed up the hole in the roof that used to let out the smoke of the fourteenth century fires. But their little pink renovating bricks are only small isolated patches among the vast sandstone blocks, and behind their panelling are the original horsehair and wattle walls.

Stephen Crane's visitors used to revel in the Gothic gloom of the place when it still had owls flying around the hall and rushes on the floor. Even between the wars Brede was still lit by candle and had no sanitation.

Roger and Alexandra Frewen really made the house luxurious for probably the first time in its six centuries of life. Comfortable four posters adorn the bedrooms, there are fitted carpets on the floors and formerly bleak rooms are now dens and nurseries for their children. But still the overriding influence in the manor comes from the year 1350 when the Black Death ravaged England and before Chaucer began to brighten up the feudal scene.

The lightest part of the house is the lovely chapel on the extreme west side, said to have been built on the site of an ancient shrine. It houses a wooden Madonna carved by Clare Sheridan, and all four of Mr. and Mrs. Frewen's children were christened there.

The priests who, for countless years, served Mass to the lords and ladies of Brede, used to reach their bedroom-cum-cell upstairs by a primitive spoked ladder, which is still in existence.

Tom's main preoccupation was with this chapel and the room above it. When we had once more settled in front of the big log fire, he said, "There is the strong influence there of a man—a priest, who can be seen at certain times of the season.

137

"You definitely have the ghost of a man and a woman who haunt the bedrooms in the east side. But they are less distinct. I should say the priest was the main influence in the house, and a very good influence."

Mr. Frewen complimented him on being perfectly right, and made us free of the writings and records on the Brede ghosts which were to prove Tom's findings to the hilt.

The first account came from a woman who, when she was young, used to spend a lot of time at Brede with Stephen Crane and his wife, Cora. It told of doors that would unlatch themselves and swing open, one after the other, and of footsteps that could clearly be heard going upstairs but never came down.

After Stephen Crane's death in 1900, Mr. and Mrs. Moreton Frewen moved back and the hauntings, or at least the accounts of the hauntings, picked up. Mrs. Moreton Frewen had been one of the lovely Jerome girls who so dazzled England with their beauty and charm when they came over from New York. It was natural therefore that she should invite her sister, Lady Randolph Churchill, to stay with her at Brede. But she made the mistake of putting her in the main guest bedroom, which was uneasily haunted. Halfway through the night Jenny Churchill came running out of the room saying that she couldn't stand it any more—and slept the rest of the night in Clara's room. The next morning she packed her bags and left and, so they say, never came back.

The trouble was that Clara Moreton Frewen was so gentle and kindly that she thought the ghosts at Brede—of which she was quite aware—were the same. It was true that Sir Winston Churchill whenever he visited his aunt would sleep the night through, sweetly and untroubled—but then, he always did.

The effect of the house on other people was less restful.

Clare Sheridan paid long and frequent visits to her parents at Brede after the death of her husband in the trenches, bringing with her her son Richard and her daughter Margaret.

In her book, *Morning Glory* (Longmans) written under her pen name of Mary Motley, Margaret Sheridan has described how she used to dread those visits because she was so frightened by Brede's atmosphere. And if anyone should have been used to ghosts it was Margaret Sheridan —she had her first experience of one at the age of three, and had been completely unafraid.

In *Morning Glory* she describes how everyone at Frampton, the Sheridan home, was waiting anxiously for news from the front where her father was to lead a frontal attack on the German lines.

"A few days earlier, on my way down to the drawing-room at tea time, I met a little boy on the stairs. He was wearing a white sailor suit, with a round straw hat on the back of his head.

"He looked at me, and I looked at him. We passed each other without a word. Nanny had always impressed upon me that I must never speak to strangers; I assumed, nevertheless, that he had come to play with me.

"As soon as I got into the drawing-room, I announced with shrill anticipation, 'I saw an itty sailor boy'. I waited for an explanation. 'An itty sailor boy', I repeated.

"In the ashen silence which followed, my grandmother directed my attention to the dish of buttered toast. Her hands were trembling.

"I was not to know, until much later, that the sailor boy was a visitor of ill-omen in the Sheridan family. In life he was an ancestor who had been drowned at sea as a midshipman. He appeared at Frampton only before the death of an heir.

"The strange part was that the portrait of him was that of a young man of sixteen or seventeen, yet what I saw— and saw clearly—was a child about my own age.

"Shortly afterwards the letter came."

Less clearly seen though they were, the ghosts at Brede were more terrifying to the young Margaret Sheridan than this visitation had ever been. She used to lie in bed at night praying that the voices coming up from the dining-room below, would go on for ever. But eventually the family would get up from table and go into the drawing-room where she couldn't hear them—and the "hideous atmosphere" of Brede would have her at its mercy.

She wasn't helped by the fact that everybody in the house believed in the ghosts. Her own mother most certainly did. So did her Uncle "Peter" —the naval officer, Oswald Frewen, who had gone through the Battle of Jutland without turning a hair, but who refused to enter certain rooms at night. Her other uncle, Hugh—the present owner's father—had once appeared white and trembling from the cellar and refused to discuss what he had seen down there. And as for her grandfather, Moreton Frewen, an Edwardian of the grand manner— he was nicknamed "Mortal Ruin" by the friends who knew of his daring, and sometimes disastrous, financial deals— he could bluff it out as much as he liked, but he still refused to cross a certain section of the garden at night without someone coming with him.

Margaret's greatest bugbear was the "something that met you in the porch", which more than one visitor had commented on. And when, one day, her grandfather collapsed near the porch and never recovered consciousness, Margaret's fear of the place crystallised.

In 1912, in an attempt to find out more about her dear

ghosts, Clara Frewen invited down Mr. A. P. Sinnett, the Vice-President of the Theosophical Society.

Her grandson still has the letter Sinnett wrote to her on his return, and it is interesting to see how closely it corresponds to Tom's findings. He mentions a woman in the east wing, and, corresponding to Tom's "priest", he wrote: "There is an old man who frequents the place. He lived there some hundreds of years ago and he is fond of the house. He, it appears, took notice of me from my first arrival, recognising me as connected with the occult world in which he was deeply interested in life, and I am told that when I was out of the body in sleep I had a long talk with him.

"He is altogether friendly to you and the family and endeavours to be helpful to you, by carrying to your sons the thought forms which your love for them engenders. This may not be very intelligible to you, but some day when you are up in London I might be able to see you and talk it all over."

Tom described him as a priest. A. P. Sinnett as a friendly old man. But it was Clare Sheridan, that amazing sculptress, traveller and writer, who became his friend and described him in detail.

Left a widow with two children while still a young and attractive woman, Clare Sheridan first hit the headlines when, not long after the Revolution, she went to Russia to model the heads of men like Lenin and Trotsky. She came back thrilled by the Russians and declaring socialist tendencies which shocked the more staid of her friends. Clare, however, didn't care what people thought as long as she was allowed to continue with her sculpture.

A few years later she was off again—this time to live and work among the Blackfeet Indians in America. After that, with her two young children, Margaret and Dick, in tow, she blazed across Eastern Europe, conquering all difficulties by her charm and vitality, eventually ending up in the quiet of the Algerian desert.

In September, 1936, on his twenty-first birthday, her son Richard inherited Frampton, the Sheridan estate. Two months later, after an appendix operation, he died in Algeria.

Broken hearted, and with much of her vitality gone, Clare Sheridan returned to Brede to try and find solace in old memories. She let the old house, and, instead, she built herself a studio house in the park and there she stayed, on the outskirts of her own home. Her strange and compelling book, *My Crowded Sanctuary* (Methuen), tells the story of this time.

Gradually she became aware of the fact that she was sharing Brede with an unseen company of spirits, among them her own son, with whom, she says, she was in constant contact.

With a medium friend she made their acquaintance.

First there was Martha, who haunted a dell in the grounds. Clare Sheridan said that Martha, with whom she frequently communed, was a Tudor maidservant who was hanged from a tree in the dell by her master for stealing. And there are grounds for believing that Mrs. Sheridan was right. What is certain is that when the Frewens came to live at Brede they found it necessary to have Martha exorcised.

The trouble was that Martha's dell adjoined a cattle gate crossing a private road on the estate, which car drivers had to open before they could proceed.

In *My Crowded Sanctuary* Clare Sheridan writes: "For me, the immense importance resulting from knowing Martha was that my fear of the upper gate after dark, and the dell, was instantly eliminated. The gate is now called after her.

No one ever thinks of describing it by any other name. Whether people know about Martha or disbelieve in her makes no difference; the gate is Martha's Gate. Never do I go through it without hailing her. She is not always there, though generally I am aware that she is. Again and again I tell her, half wearily, half jokingly, as I hitch back the gate, 'Oh, Martha! I wish you could open it for me,' to which Martha wistfully rejoins, 'I wish I could'. Peter (Clare Sheridan's brother) also repeatedly reiterated, 'If only Martha . . .' and it would certainly not surprise either of us if one day a shyly smiling girl in lavender blue—for that is the colour I associate with Martha—opened the gate and curtsied prettily.

"Peter has asked me, when I'm leaving him after dark, 'Are you sure you're not afraid of the Martha Gate?' and I am able to reassure him in all sincerity, for Martha and I are friends, whether it's light or whether it's dark."

But while Clare Sheridan may have been able to befriend Martha, other people—even strangers to the Martha legend—found the atmosphere there so hateful after dark that nobody would get out of the car to open the gate.

But the greatest influence in Clare Sheridan's life at that time was Father John, the age-old spirit of the priest who lived in the Brede chapel. She writes: "I could not have pulled through the war years without his help."

For as well as her personal sorrow Mrs. Sheridan, during the war, also had to bear living in her eyrie in the grounds and watch the Army, which was billeted at Brede manor, methodically turn her beloved home and garden into a scarred mess.

Father John, according to her, binds himself to the chapel at Brede from choice. He is no aimless, ignorant ghost, but an appointed guide to the spirits of both the dead and the living who need aid.

143

At first Clare Sheridan discovered him through her medium friend, Shirley Eshelby. Later she was able to commune with him by herself. Mr. Roger Frewen told me, "If ever Aunt Clare comes here, she always goes into the chapel and seems to find peace in there." And his wife said, "Since we have lived here I have come to believe very firmly in Father John's existence."

In 1947, Clare was forced to sell Brede. It became the property of a Captain Ronald Traquair. Three years later he was killed in a car accident, and the house that had been a Frewen home for two hundred and fifty years was once more on the open market.

Luckily Mr. Roger Frewen, then in the diplomatic corps, heard about it and bought it back into the family.

Both Mr. Frewen and his wife, incidentally, are related to former Prime Ministers. Mr. Frewen is cousin to Sir Winston and Mrs. Frewen, a sister of Lord Selby, is a cousin of the late Lord Avon.

It is one thing to have ghost history at your fingertips. It is another to believe in them. I began to sound out the Frewens on their attitude towards the ghosts of Brede. I already had an idea that Mr. Frewen, at least, accepted them as real entities.

His letter in reply to mine said that he would be pleased to see Tom and myself, but he didn't want us to hold a seance at Brede. With several guests staying in the house, he explained, he was unwilling to have the moderately quiescent ghosts stirred up.

I couldn't blame him. Once when Clare Sheridan and Mrs. Eshelby held a two-woman seance in the oak-panelled hall at Brede they had been confronted by the violent spirit of an Oxenbridge who told them he had been stabbed in his sleep by a jealous neighbour centuries before.

The private
chapel at
Brede Place

The haunted bedroom at Buriton Manor

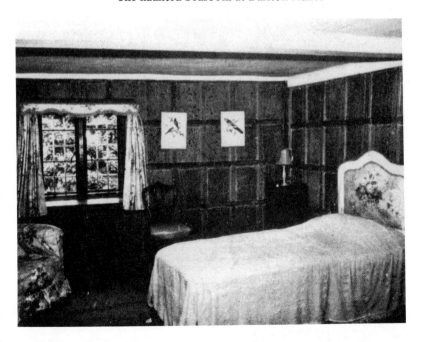

At Burford Priory with the Very Reverend Mother Prioress

I was able to write back and assure him on this, and point out the not readily appreciated differences between a medium and a clairvoyant.

Even without the accounts of their relations and friends of what had gone before, the Frewens had experienced enough since they came there to convince them of the ghosts at Brede.

One of the first things that happened occurred during the Easter holidays one year when a woman friend of theirs came to stay, bringing with her a son, who was on vacation from Harrow. Mr. Frewen told us the story:

"We put my friend in the Damasc Room, and the boy in the little room next door.

"I admit that it is a funny little room, with a frieze of gargoyles going round the wall, put there by my Uncle Peter. But that can't account for what happened.

"When the son didn't appear for breakfast we got worried and went up to see if he was all right. We found him huddled up with his head beneath the bedclothes. He said that he had been awakened in the early hours of the morning by somebody coming into the room. He thought it was probably his mother. But when he was able to see the figure by the moonlight he saw it was a woman in what he described as 'a large dress and a ruff round her neck'. He just stayed there, frozen with fright until we found him.

"And that boy wasn't given to imaginative fancies. He had been given a healthy, outdoor, practical upbringing in Kenya."

Tom had found no trace of this lady ghost. The only presence that haunted that particular part of the house was most definitely, he said, a man.

In fact, as we stood in that room on our tour of the house, he had said to me: "I have a feeling that a man was beheaded in this room."

Greatly as I admired Tom's gift, there are times when I can't help feeling that it has gone a bit off the rails. I am always proved wrong. I was this time, for, when we got downstairs Mr. Frewen showed me photographic proof of what Tom had said.

Some time after the schoolboy episode, Mr. Frewen had asked a photographer friend of his to take pictures of the inside and outside of Brede. He showed me the series of photographs that had resulted—and very beautiful they are. But one of them, which had been taken in a room near the little bedroom, had on it the smoky, transparent, but undeniable figure of a headless man.

I looked carefully at the photograph. It was unlikely, but there was a slight possibility that the figure had been caused by a freak effect of fogging.

I asked Mr. Frewen who had taken the photographs.

"A man called Johnny Silverside," he told me.

I knew then that it was almost certainly not fogging. I have known Johnny, an extremely able and talented photographer, for years. We used to work on rival Fleet Street dailies. However, to clinch the matter, when I got back to London I rang him up.

I don't know what sort of reaction I was expecting—sarcasm, I suppose. Although Johnny and I have discussed many things in many places during the endless waits that journalism entails, we have never discussed ghosts. And Fleet Street photographers are notorious cynics. But Johnny said right away: "Yes, it's most likely it was a ghost. There's nothing else that will account for it. I was surprised myself when I developed the prints and saw the figure, but I looked on the negs and there was no fogging on the rebate surround, which there would have been if the figure *had* been caused by fogging. And I tested out the slide cover which had housed those particular films

146

time and time again after that—it wasn't letting in any light.

"Myself, I'm fairly sure it was a ghost. The funny thing was that, although I'm fairly sensitive to supernatural things, I didn't feel this one.

"Once, when I had a flat in Sloane Square, a poltergeist moved in. I could be thinking about something completely different, then suddenly the hair on the back of my neck would rise so I knew it was there—and immediately things would begin to move.

"But I was going round in a terrific rush at Brede, so maybe I didn't have time to sense it."

The section of the house where Tom found the spirit of a woman contains Mr. Frewen's bedroom and the small dressing-room that leads off it.

"It used to be my grandmother's room," he said. "And the little one leading off it was her secret place, forbidden to us children and, as far as I know, nobody else went in to it.

"One night I went in there—it wasn't long after we'd installed ourselves and been working very hard to get the place up to its best. Suddenly as I stood there, came the scent of violets—quite strongly. It was exactly the scent that my grandmother had used all her life, and I knew she was there, watching me and trying to tell me she approved of all we had done for her old home."

His wife, busy though she was — after having brought up four children she ran Brede's 400 acres of farmland when her husband was away — had time to experience the same thing.

"In many ways this is an eerie house," she said. "There are so many hidden presences around. For instance, there is a carpet at the foot of the main stairs, placed over the site of the old altar, which is constantly being moved.

"I'm always putting into place and, when I come back some time later, I find it has shifted again. Time and again I've tested this phenomenon out—putting it straight and making quite sure that nobody is on hand to move it—but always it is in a different position when I return a few minutes later." The rug, incidentally, is at the top of the stairs which lead to the cellar, where Mr. Frewen's father became so frightened.

Recently, Mr. Frewen has written to me to say that he has found out that the rug is a Moslem prayer mat. As a result, feeling that a Moslem rug may not like lying on the site of a Christian altar, he has replaced it with a more ordinary Persian carpet, which, so far, hasn't moved.

Apart from this rather niggling mystery, Mrs. Frewen found that of other presences in the house, two at least gave her considerable comfort.

"One is Father John, and, as I say, I know he is here. Then there is Roger's grandmother, Mrs. Moreton Frewen. She died just six months before I was born, yet I feel that I know her very well.

"I am sure she helped me when I was furnishing the house. I couldn't seem to go into a shop without finding some piece of furniture that had once belonged to Brede—it was the most amazing thing. And often when I am working in the garden among the roses, which were her pride and joy, I feel she is there.

"I know she is haunting Brede and I'm terribly pleased about it."

TEN

Burford Priory

❉   ❉

BURFORD IS A strange little town. Its beauty's fame has crowded its hilly main street with visitors from all over the world. It offers good food served in some of the most beautiful inns in the Cotswolds, and olde worlde tea shops that really are olde worlde.

Yet Burford has never sold out to the tourist. Its houses and secret walled gardens retain their dignity and convey the impression that it was not always just a pretty face, but had been a town of some consequence long before the first tourist went ga-ga over it.

And indeed it was. It was an important feather in the cap of Wessex when England was divided into rival states. One of the many Synods which tried to decide the date of Easter was held there in A.D. 685. Fifty years later Ethelbald, king of Mercia, decided it was worth conquering and marched on it from the east. But the Army of Wessex met him on the banks of the sleepy Windrush and after a battle that made its waters run red, drove him back. The town was at its most prosperous from the mid-thirteenth to the early sixteenth centuries as a centre for cloth and paper-making, and much of its lovely stone work dates from the 1450s.

Where there is that amount of history there will, usually, be a proportionate amount of ghosts. I am told that more than one Burford resident has an odd tale to tell. But this book is about houses in particular and we would have passed over Burford if it hadn't been for a friend of Tom Corbett's who said to him one day, "Why don't you visit Burford Priory? I believe that is very haunted."

The Priory certainly qualifies as a stately home. Although it now belonged to an enclosed order of nuns, it has a long secular history during which it was very stately indeed.

However, I had my doubts about receiving permission to investigate it. Convents do not usually throw open their doors to clairvoyants. But I had reckoned without the kindness of the Very Reverend Mother Prioress who said she would be pleased to allow us to visit the Priory. In fact, she went on: "We are puzzled at certain happenings, and will welcome any light on the subject."

.   .   .   .   .

There is no record of when the Hospital of St. John the Evangelist, later known as The Priory, began its work at Burford. It was probably already old when a royal gift of firewood was made to it in 1226—the first time it crops up in any records.

It was a poor, independent foundation where a Master and three brethren of the Augustinian rule cared for the sick and looked after needy travellers.

The presentation to the Mastership was in the hands of the Lords of Burford, one of whom was Warwick the Kingmaker, and it is in this connection that Burford records possess one of the only two specimens of his signature known to exist.

By the Dissolution, the Priory had become more or less a sinecure where old priests were pastured out. What little land and property it had was leased to tenants.

What Burford thought of its Priory at this time we don't really know. But from the Reformation onwards there came a schism between it and the town. Even now the Priory, behind its gates at the top of Priory Lane, gives the appearance of standing aloof and having little contact with the life of the community, which, in view of its history, is not surprising.

In 1543, Henry VIII granted the property to Edward Harman, his barber-surgeon, who probably never lived there—leaving it empty and suspended, away from the bustle of the town.

The next owner widened the gap further. He was Sir Lawrence Tanfield, Lord Chief Baron of the Exchequer, who may have been a wizard with finance but had no gift for winning friends. He was cordially disliked by the people of Burford, and at Great Tew, where he had another estate.

He built a fine Elizabethan house on the site of the old Hospital and had the imagination to incorporate many of the twelfth-century features of that old building in it. But he insisted on recovering all the old manorial rights which had gradually passed over to the town—an action that alienated forever any affection the Corporation might have had for him.

Tanfield was also accused in Parliament of abusing his power as Lord of the manor to enclose seven areas of the best pasture land in the neighbourhood. Another accusation was that he didn't pay his church dues. Nevertheless, James I knighted him at the Priory after a hunting visit during which he was well feasted.

So it was some relief to the town when in 1637 the Priory passed out of the loathed Tanfield hands and into those of William Lenthall, the great Speaker of the Long Parliament.

If he had never done anything else Lenthall would be remembered for what he told Charles I when that King had rushed into the House of Commons, demanding to know where five members of it had gone to: "I have, Sir, neither eyes to see, nor tongue to speak in this place, but as the House is pleased to direct me, whose servant I am."

Lenthall enlarged the Priory and added an elegant little chapel to its frontage. After his death, the Priory went to William's son, John, who had managed to hunt with the Cromwellian hounds, but later ran with the Restoration hare and went down in history with the title conferred on him by Antony Wood: "The grand Braggadochio and Lyar of the age he lived in."

However, during John's lifetime Charles II condescended to visit the Priory—presumably dragging our old friend Nell along, since one of the bedrooms was ever after "Nell Gwynne's room", and still, presumably, gaining inspiration for titles to confer upon their son because besides being the Duke of St. Albans, the boy also became the Earl of Burford.

The next royal visit was made by William III to the wife of John Lenthall's son and her second husband Lord Abercorn, in 1695. Two years later, Lord Abercorn was put on trial for the murder of one of his stepsons' trustees, John Pryor, with whom he had quarrelled. Pryor had been found dead in the Priory grounds. But Abercorn was acquitted and, as one history casually put it, "a gardener was hanged instead."

The Lenthalls owned the Priory until 1828, but it is significant that those of them who owned two estates always preferred the other to the Priory, which gradually became mortgaged, split up and vastly reduced in size.

The Lenthalls sold the estate to a Mr. Giles Greenaway of Little Barrington. Now until he bought the Priory Mr.

Greenaway and his son had been very friendly with a Sir Biddulph Martin with whom the son had gone through Oxford. When the Greenaways moved into the Priory, Sir Biddulph—not wanting to lose contact with his great friends—bought the estate next door. The boundary between the two properties was marked by the River Windrush.

After that their friendship lasted just one week. For, so the story goes, in that time the two families quarrelled bitterly about the Windrush fishing rights—and never spoke to each other again.

After that the Priory went into Chancery, at a time when Dickens, in *Bleak House*, was attacking that legal system for the ruinously slow way it worked. But the mills of Chancery went on grinding regardless of Dickens and the place became desperately neglected, almost a ruin, and had by now acquired such a reputation that the townsfolk avoided it altogether.

In 1908 a new owner bought it and repaired it. From then on it passed from hand to hand until it became the property of Sir Archibald Southby, the former Tory M.P. for Epsom, and at one time a Government Whip. His and Lady Southby's ownership of the Priory was marked by a series of calamities, culminating at the end of the war when Sir Archibald visited the Nazi concentration camp of Buchenwald as a member of a Parliamentary delegation. At Buchenwald Sir Archibald picked up an illness that enforced his retirement and, eventually, the sale of his home.

The Priory was never a happy house. Lady Southby told the Mother Prioress that she and her husband had decided that it would never be completely at rest until it went back to the church. She mentioned that it was restlessly haunted. So in 1947 the Southbys handed the Priory and its sixteen acres of woodland over to the Anglo-Catholic Church and the twenty-one sisters of the contemplative Benedictine order of the Salutation of the Blessed Virgin Mary moved in.

The gentle sisters found a very different house from the one that Lord Tanfield built. Only the south wing and the chapel remains. On the east side lies the walled rose garden, at the back and to the west stretch sixteen acres of woodland where the Windrush winds through the shade and where the Regency Lenthalls had their bathing pool.

Immediately on the right of the entrance gates, and shielded from the big house by the tall yew hedge, is the old Rectory, which has been divided into three sections, one for the convent's chaplain, one for visitors and the other for the gardener and his wife. It was here, the Reverend Mother told us, that the most troubling happenings had occurred.

In fact, she said, the supernatural events that pestered the whole convent could be neatly divided into two—the ones at the Rectory which were disturbing, and the ones at the Priory itself, which, somehow, were not.

She dealt first with the Priory.

"The first unusual event took place very soon after we came here," she said. "One of the sisters was in the garden where we had put a big cage to protect some young plants from the cats. She saw coming from the woods and walking straight towards the cage what she described as a man dressed like an old-fashioned gamekeeper. He was carrying an old type of gun under his arm.

"He kept on coming straight for the cage and she began to be afraid he hadn't seen it and would trip over it. She went up to him to warn him, but he had reached it. And then she saw that he was going straight through it. After that he disappeared."

Later, Tom was to look for this apparition in the garden, but he didn't find him. It seems likely, however, that he was the poor gardener who was "hanged instead" after the Abercorn trial. The dreadfulness of being "hanged instead" would surely be enough to make anyone haunt. However, the gentle influence of the nuns and their prayers seems to have helped him find rest, because he has not been seen since 1949.

The entrance hall at the Priory is a huge, stone-flagged chamber, warmed by a great Tudor fireplace. On the left are two big arches. Colonel La Terrière, who was the owner between 1908 and 1912, found them incorporated between the hall and the study, unbricked them and let them stand. They are probably part of the original Hospital.

The entrance hall is quite definitely haunted. Tom sensed that the moment he came in, and mentioned it when we were shown into the Mother Prioress's study, another lovely room with Tudor mullioned windows that leads directly off the hall.

"That's very clever of you, Mr. Corbett," said the Mother Prioress. "Lady Southby told us that people coming to the Priory had, quite frequently, seen a little brown monk around the place, and he has been detected in the hall.

"We began to notice it when a Professor from Oxford, a relative of one of our sisters, came to visit her. While he was waiting for her, he sat in the hall. When she arrived he said, 'Who was that nun dressed in brown? I thought you all wore black here. She came into the hall and stood by the fireplace, then she walked away.'"

Here Tom interrupted. "But what I found in the hall was a man, not a woman," he said.

"We have come to think that may be right," the Mother

Prioress told him. "The professor saw a figure with its head covered by a cowl. Since he was in a convent he naturally assumed it was a nun.

"There's definitely something very strange about that entrance hall. Time and again somebody comes to the door of my study here and knocks. I can't tell you how many times this happens. When I get to the door and open it, there is nobody there at all. And a priest who came to see us and was given lunch in the hall in solitary state told us afterwards that all the time he had the uncomfortable feeling that someone was watching him.

"Then the professor came again. And again, believe it or not, he saw the brown-clad figure. He said it walked in exactly as before and went to the fireplace, and then came to my office. He noticed that it made absolutely no noise at all as it walked. He didn't think it was one of us that time.

"Then, two years ago, a lady visitor came to vespers with us, at the chapel. She stood up there looking out on to the front lawn where our gardener was mowing the lawn. Suddenly she saw, standing right in front of the path of the mower a monk. She says he was in brown, quite young, and he was apparently deep in thought. Neither he nor the gardener seemed aware of the other. In fact she called out because the gardener was aiming straight at him and seemed about to knock the monk down with the mower.

"But, she said, just as the mower reached him, he disappeared."

There seem no boundaries to the monk's appearance. He has been seen on the front lawn, in the entrance hall, in the chapel and in the corridor outside the nuns' cells.

The Reverend Mother led us on a tour of inspection as far as she could without infringing on the rule of the enclosure, which is a part of the convent where no man may enter—although the ghostly, brown-clad monk does not seem aware of this law.

In the thin November sun, we strolled down through the bare trees to the Windrush over which the Greenaways and Sir Biddulph broke up a friendship. Through these woods once ran an old coaching road. Now its modern equivalent runs well to the north so that Burford is blessedly free of roaring exhausts.

We passed through the door in an old brick wall into the sheltered rose garden where the lawn lies in beautifully-tended steps. At the top, in the north-east corner, is the burial ground of the monks who lived here from the time of King Richard I to Henry VIII. It is here, in a little summer-house, that the body of the murdered Mr. Pryor was supposed to have been found.

The rose garden is bounded on the south by the colonnade which leads from the Priory to the chapel. This damp, cold, but beautifully designed, chapel was built under the supervision of Speaker Lenthall and consecrated in 1662 by a bishop who described it as "a most elegant piece".

Families at the Priory have worshipped there ever since, and when it was investigated recently it was found that beneath the altar was a stone coffin of very great age. But its dampness has made it unsuitable for the use of the nuns, especially in the winter months, and they have made a chapel for themselves in a high room of the Priory overlooking the rose garden.

It is approached from the east by the open-air terrace built on top of the colonnade, that leads from the old chapel to the new.

As we left Lenthall's chapel and climbed the open stairway to the terrace, I was walking on ahead with the Mother Prioress. Tom and Jeremy Grayson were bringing up the rear. Suddenly, I heard them stop, and when I looked back they were both staring back at the empty chapel we had left. "Did you hear it?" Tom asked me. "Hear what?"

"I heard it," said Jeremy, "it was the sound of voices singing back in the chapel. Only for an instant. It sounded like part of a service."

The Mother Prioress, who takes everything in her stride, was not surprised. "Other people have told me they have heard singing from the chapel before," she said.

She went on to tell us that the walk we were on at the moment was haunted. "Something seems to come along here and enter the chapel that we use in the Priory. It enters through this door."

We went through the little doorway out of the cold wind and into a high room with tall mullion windows and a magnificent Catherine of Aragon ceiling, where the nuns have raised an altar and installed pews for a small congregation. As we stood and looked towards the altar we were at the bottom of the room in a little passageway that leads from the terrace to the robing room.

"Very often—so many times that I have lost count," says the Reverend Mother—"when the nuns are kneeling at their devotions during morning office they hear the door coming from the terrace open and close, and footsteps proceed along the little passageway to the robing room. At first we always thought it was the chaplain coming to take service, and we waited for his appearance. And then, about ten minutes later, the real chaplain came in from the terrace door and crossed to the robing room.

"It's always happening. We think the chaplain has come because we hear him arrive. But it isn't him. He arrives later. Who it is who comes in first and goes to the robing room, we don't know because we've never seen him."

Tom looked puzzled. "Haven't you ever seen a ghost up

by the altar?" he asked. Reverend Mother smiled. "As a matter of fact we have," she said. "I myself have twice seen a brown figure kneeling up there. I've watched it for several minutes, then when I've turned away and looked again it has gone."

Probably one of the strangest manifestations in the Priory is the ringing of the bell. It peals loudly through the silent convent at two o'clock, which is when the medieval monks of Burford were called to chapel for the first office of the day.

"There is, of course, nobody ringing it," said the Reverend Mother. "Some of us hear it, others don't. It was ringing very loudly and violently the other night when one of the sisters heard a tap on the door of her room. She had been awakened by the bell, so she got up and opened the door. Outside she saw the profile of a figure. At first she thought it was me. She says it was about my height and wearing robes and was hooded. And in the dark the robe looked black. But when she spoke to it, it disappeared.

"This has happened to her several times. Last summer she saw it in daylight and saw it was a monk. She said: 'Can I help you?' "

Tom nodded his approval. "That," he said, "was exactly the right thing to do—talk to him. It establishes a sort of contact, and very often it seems to diminish a ghost's restlessness."

The Mother Prioress went on: "The funniest thing about the bell, though, was when four postulants came to the convent. The first night they were here we heard a commotion and came to find out that all four of them had got up and dressed. They said they had heard the rising bell. It was exactly two o'clock in the morning."

The nuns take the happenings at the Priory with calmness. The Mother Prioress did not tell us what she thought about them but was obviously unafraid and unruffled. Tom told her that he, too, thought there was nothing to worry about. "I believe that one of the monks who once lived here has appointed himself as guardian to the place," he said. "He is still carrying out the ceremonies he carried out in life—the ringing of the bell to office, the praying by the altar. I think he is happy that the house has been returned to the worship of God. He is an old inhabitant. There will be no more unhappiness in the house again."

The haunting of the Old Rectory is a different matter. This has disturbed the sisters so much that only the week before our visit they had held a Requiem service in one of the rooms there to calm the restlessness that was disturbing the house.

The Old Rectory is divided into three. One section for the chaplain, one for the gardener and his wife and one for visitors.

A year and a week before our visit the chaplain's section had been left empty for a time and two of the nuns had moved in there to sleep until the chaplain returned.

"One of them was in a room directly below the other's," said the Mother Prioress. "Just after eleven she was woken up by the sound of heavy · footsteps overhead. They tramped up and down intermittently until about two." The next morning she asked the sister who had been in the room above her if she had been ill during the night. The sister was very surprised and said she hadn't got out of bed once.

"It happened again the next night and the next night.

"It occurred again this year, but since the Requiem mass everything has been quiet."

By this time we were walking down the little cobbled path that leads from the Priory to the Old Rectory.

The trouble, whatever it is, has not been confined to the

chaplain's part of the house. A visitor in one of the neat, bare little bedrooms has had her hot water bottle taken away from her and thrown out of the door by an unseen agency. On another occasion the gardener and his wife who live in the next section and are not, according to the Reverend Mother "an over-imaginative couple", heard a high scream coming from one of the attics. They said it was as if someone was being murdered in there. Yet the room was unoccupied at the time. In another bedroom a monk has been seen.

Tom was most interested in the attic from which the scream had come. He stood there for a long time in the centre of the room while we waited to hear what he had to say. The sunlight was having a struggle to get in under the low eaves. Then he turned to the Mother Prioress. "Have you any idea what this house, or the original house that stood on this site, was used for in the days of the old Hospital?" he asked her.

She shook her head.

"Because I think," went on Tom, "that part of it at least was a sort of punishment block. There is a tremendous feeling of unexpiated guilt here. And in one of the bed-rooms where there is a low beam across the ceiling, I got the image of someone either flogging himself or being flogged. And in this attic I'm afraid that someone was murdered or some equally terrible crime took place. The monks of those days were not all they should be.

"But I think that the Requiem released the worst that was here. You were perfectly right to treat the ghosts as real entities who need rest. There is no good in ignoring the sort of happenings you have been having here."

The dining-room in the visitors' quarters was another part of the Rectory that the Mother Prioress wanted Tom to have a look at. It appeared an unexceptionable little room but it was, she told us, a place where things kept disappearing.

"The most amazing disappearance," said the Mother Prioress, "was when I was entertaining one of our lady visitors to lunch in here. There was a dish of ham on the sideboard, covered by a plate. I picked it up to serve our visitor and the top plate literally flew out of my hand. I stooped to pick it up, expecting to find it shattered at my feet. But there was nothing there. No plate, no pieces— nothing. Both of us immediately searched the room which, as you see, is small. But we never found those pieces. They had just disappeared."

"You know, of course, that it was a ghost," said Tom. "It was obviously a silly and malicious joke on its part. It is all connected with the trouble you have had with this whole house, probably caused by one and the same ghost.

"I think you have acted exactly right in holding a requiem for it, and that most of the trouble is now over. But even so, if I were you, I wouldn't put anyone of an impressionable, sensitive temperament in the most haunted rooms. Such people can be influenced."

He explained his theory that, while ghosts do not have the power to do actual harm, they can be the deciding factor that turns something already bad into something worse. "They can tip minds that are already balanced on a mental tightrope over the edge," said Tom. "I often wonder, when I hear of sudden, violent, inexplicable murders, whether the murderer wasn't finally pushed into it by having been in contact with unseen malevolence.

"However, the dominating influence in this house here is that of guilt. Somebody, a man, has committed a grave sin here and isn't finding it easy to forgive himself."

He made no attempt to explain how the plate had managed to disappear as it had because he did not know.

"There's no doubt that ghosts can sometimes take physical action like lifting and taking away a plate, or opening a door," he said. "But their activities are very limited in this direction and, I imagine, take up a good deal of ecto-plasmic energy."

If the happenings at the Old Rectory were an untidy jumble of guilt and maliciousness which resulted in an equally untidy hotch-potch of disappearing objects, screams and a very real atmosphere of trouble, the hap-penings at the Priory had a much clearer pattern. Once again, we had come up against a guardian-figure of a ghost, who was drawn back again and again to his old ground by a care for it.

There is no doubt that the unhappiness and ruin that had come to the Priory had brought about a vicious circle of restlessness and misery, causing an atmosphere that had brought on more restlessness and more misery. But that has now receded under the influence of the nuns, and what remains is the solitary spirit of an old inhabitant going quietly about the business of monastic life, as he did when he was alive.

Strangely enough, we were to encounter almost exactly similar circumstances—although on a very much larger and more dramatic scale—at the very next house we visited, Beaulieu, the home of Lord Montagu.

But, for all the peace and calm that is gradually seeping back into the Priory, it will still be a long time before it gets rid of that sense of isolation that surrounds it and sepa ates it from the pleasant little town it stands in, and which began over four hundred years ago, when it was taken away from the monks to whom it belonged.

ELEVEN

Beaulieu

IF THERE IS an absence of Tom Corbett in this, the last chapter dealing with a specific house, it is because we visited a home where, for the first time, he found himself superfluous.

The large majority of the fifty men and women who serve and administer Beaulieu, the Hampshire home of Lord Montagu, had no need of his confirmation that it was haunted. They knew that already—and how, and by whom. Too many people have seen the monks of Beaulieu too many times to permit doubt in any but the most sceptical mind.

This is not to say that there are more ghosts at Beaulieu than anywhere else—there are just more people around to see them. The whole estate of 9,000 acres, its farms, its historical and motor museums, its jazz festivals and car rallies, and its tremendous popularity with the public has an extremely large staff resident on the estate—and the bigger the population, the bigger its incidence of psychics.

However it is, we have never encountered such a mass of evidence from any one stately home as we encountered at Beaulieu. From the time we arrived, soon after lunch, to the time we left, long after dark, Tom, Jeremy and myself were kept spinning like tops around the estate, trying to keep up with the schedule of visits laid on for us by Lord Montagu to people who had relevant information to give.

It is sufficient to say that Tom confirmed them all.

Almost as fascinating as the information was the casual attitude with which most Beaulieu-ites gave it. When Lord Montagu met us at the door and took us into his office for the briefing, he said, "You'll find that ghosts are an accepted part of the scene here. In the village their attitude is 'Yes, we see the monks; so what?' "

He was perfectly right. My question, "So you believe in ghosts, then?" was received more often than not with a blank stare. You don't believe or disbelieve in the obvious —you merely take it for granted.

I have left out a lot of material that was so kindly given to me because, for one thing, there just isn't the space and, for another, it was mainly repetitive. But I do realise that the haunting of Beaulieu really deserves a book to itself and by trying to compress it into one chapter I am merely skimming the surface of a deep vat.

· · · · ·

The monks first came to Beaulieu in 1204, when King John, who had primarily given them a Royal Manor in Berkshire, decided to transfer them further south to a spot in the New Forest at the head of the tidal waters of Beaulieu river.

There were thirty of them under an abbot, all belonging to the Cistercian order. The mother house of the Cistercians was—and still is—the Abbey of Citeaux which broke away from the Benedictines in 1098, in order to observe the Benedictine rule more strictly.

Austerity and manual labour were the order of their day. They had to live in a remote place, far away from any lay dwellings and to concentrate on simplicity in their lives and possessions. They were woken at frequent intervals during the night to attend services, beginning at 2 a.m. They had just two minutes to get out of bed, dress and get to the chapel to sing office. No woman was allowed to lodge in any monastery belonging to them, but other travellers were to be lodged and treated as if they were Our Lord himself.

It is important to remember, in order to understand what follows, that the Cistercian abbot wore white, his choir monks also wore a white robe which, when working, they covered with a black scapula, and the lay brothers wore brown.

These lay brothers were recruited from all ranks of society to carry out the rougher work of the abbey. For the most part they were illiterate, barred from taking Holy Orders, and lived strictly separate from the choir monks.

With the granting of the estate, the monks of Beaulieu were also given a gift of £1,500—the equivalent of £60,000 today—to build their abbey. This and other moneys, raised by skilful acquisition of property, enabled them to erect a large number of beautiful buildings. There was the Abbey Church itself, the Domus Conversorum, where the lay brothers lived, and the Great Gatehouse where guests were received. The last two are still standing. The Domus is now Beaulieu's restaurant and the Gate-house forms the nucleus of Palace House, where Lord Montagu has made his home. Then there were the Outer Gatehouse, which is still in use as a lodge; the Refectory, now the Parish church; the wine press, the infirmary and all the other adjuncts of medieval monastic life.

The brothers were able and industrious. They made a profitable concern out of raising sheep and practised agriculture and forestry. John, their royal founder, had won their loyalty and when, in 1206, he began to wage a bloodless war against Pope Innocent III, over the appointment of a new Archbishop of Canterbury, they supported their king as best they could. They defied the Pope's interdict which he laid on England in 1208—silencing the monastery bells, closing the doors of the churches against the congregation and suffering the dead to be buried in unconsecrated ground without the benefit of last communion—by carrying on as usual.

However, in 1209 the Pope excommunicated John and threatened the same damnation to the monks who supported him, and Beaulieu was forced to obey.

During the years that followed the monks managed to acquire wealth and two distinctive rights. One was the ownership of the Beaulieu river bed—a title that has come down to the present day and makes Lord Montagu one of the very few owners of the bed of a tidal river in Britain.

The other was the right of sanctuary. People fleeing from justice or persecution could step inside the boundaries of Beaulieu and no secular authority was allowed to lay a finger on them. After that they had three choices: return and face trial, go into permanent exile or, if the monks allowed them, stay at Beaulieu for the rest of their lives.

The War of the Roses brought a noble crop of sanctuary-seekers to Beaulieu. One was the queen of Henry VI, Margaret of Anjou, who later slipped down the river and across to France to avoid the Yorkist forces.

The other was the Countess of Warwick, the King-maker's wife, who sought sanctuary at Beaulieu after her husband's death on Barnet Field. Despite the monastic law which allowed no woman to live in the abbey, the Countess stayed there for fourteen years until the accession of Henry VII restored her lands to her.

Even before they arrived at Beaulieu, the Cistercians

had begun to relax some of their most basic rules. Despite their vow of poverty and simplicity, they accepted the gift of a gold chalice from King John, and it is known that the abbot of that time used silver vessels. Gradually the raising of the standard of living went on in monasteries everywhere, leading eventually to a general galloping corruption which gave Henry VIII his excuse for the Dissolution.

The feeling of the people had turned against the monasteries some time before. Several years before the Dissolution, a pamphlet entitled "The Supplication of the Beggars" made its appearance, exhorting the King to take the monasteries into his own hands. It complained against the "holy and idle beggars and vagabonds" and the greedy extortion of the monasteries, ending: "Who is she that will set her hands to work to get 3d. a day, and may have at least 20d. a day to sleep an hour with a friar, a monk or priest?"

In 1536, Henry, with an eye to his coffers, gave in gracefully and began the Dissolution. On the whole monasteries were not too badly treated. Here and there the King ordered executions—as at Woburn. But in all about 5,000 monks, 1,600 friars and 2,000 nuns were granted pensions which actually got paid.

There is no reason to suppose that Beaulieu had been guilty of any of the grosser indulgences which had aroused the people's anger. Certainly Henry treated it as well as any. On April 2, 1538, the monks of Beaulieu signed the deed of surrender to the King fairly amicably, and in return the abbot was given a pension of £66 13s. 4d. a year, and seventeen of his monks were granted an annual income of between £4 and £5.

On July 29 of the same year, Henry VIII sold the estate to Thomas Wriothesley, the first Earl of Southampton, for £1,350 6s. 8d. It was, incidentally, this Earl's grandson, Henry, who earned the gratitude of the world by becoming patron to a contemporary playwright called William Shakespeare.

Although Beaulieu has passed through many hands since then—it became Montagu property in 1673—it has managed to avoid being split up or despoiled. In modern times, always the danger point for the great houses, it has been lucky enough to have had three generations of Montagu owners who have cared for it as a permanent home.

The Manor is still the "beautiful place" it was in King John's day—a fortress of fertile, tended land, woods and rivers surrounded on three sides by a great Monastic Bank and bounded on the other by the Solent.

John, second Baron Montagu, who was the present owner's father, built Beaulieu into a settled community by raising residential houses on the estate—all beautifully sited among the woods and fields. When he died in 1929 a tablet was set up above his grave: "He loved Beaulieu, deeming his possession of it a sacred trust to be handed on to his successors in like manner". From then on his wife, Pearl, was head of Beaulieu until 1951 when their son, Edward, inherited.

During the war, Beaulieu was one of the most important centres of wartime activity in Britain, although very few people knew it. Several of the large houses on the estate were taken over by the Special Operations Executive which trained foreign and English agents who were going to be dropped into Nazi-occupied territory to help the Resistance. The course at Beaulieu provided the "finishing off" of a long and brutally hard period of training.

While Lord Montagu was a schoolboy at Eton there were often as many as 100 agents living in his houses on and around the manor. Here, amid the quiet countryside, they learned to take on new identities; repeated endlessly the details of a fictitious childhood, family and background so that there would be no slip ups under questioning. It was from here that Odette Churchill and Violette Szabo, both later awarded the George Cross, set out for their work in France. Odette survived torture and imprisonment to come back again, but Violette was eventually executed at Ravensbruck in 1945.

When Lord Montagu inherited, he made himself a flat in Palace House, where he and his wife now live. In 1952 he opened Beaulieu to the public, and, in memory of his father who was a great pioneer motorist, he opened the Montagu Motor Museum, which has become a mechanical Mecca for everybody interested in the history of cars. Under his guidance Beaulieu has become, next to Woburn, the most-visited home in England. Like Woburn, however, the yearly invasion of about 340,000 people has not been able to frighten away the ghosts. . . .

. . . . .

Lord Montagu himself has never seen a ghost, but he accepts them as calmly and completely as anyone else at Beaulieu. Only the night before, he told us on our arrival, he had been entertaining guests to dinner in his dining-room, which was once the Gatehouse upper chapel, when there came a sudden, strong smell of incense—quite a common occurrence at Beaulieu.

"The ghosts here have never been evil," he said. "In fact, they've never been anything but extremely friendly, and they have been seen and heard by countless people."

The amazing thing is that, despite the numbers of people who have experienced the haunting, their stories of what they saw or heard have remained rigidly consistent.

Visually, it has always taken the same form—the ghost of a monk in brown. It has been seen in many different places, but it has always been a monk and always in brown, indicating that he was one of the Beaulieu lay brothers.

As well as this there is an auditory haunting. It takes the form of chanting, such as is done by monks at office. It only takes place at night, echoing clearly across the lawns of Beaulieu as it used to seven centuries ago. More often than not, it occurs after the death of someone in the village or on the estate.

"There used to be other ghosts around," said Lord Montagu. "You know, the usual type of thing—Grey Ladies and such—but they disappeared when electric light was installed."

Before he got on to the subject of the main haunting, however, Lord Montagu told us about what he believes were two supernatural incidents that happened at Beaulieu. The first bears an uncanny resemblance to the "swan" incident at Longleat—except that this time, the swans brought *good* news.

"My father married in 1890," he said. "Naturally enough, he badly wanted a son. He had five daughters, and it wasn't until 1926, thirty-six years after his first marriage, that I was born.

"They say that at the very moment of my birth the swans came up from the pond and the river and flew round and round the house.

"The other incident was even stranger. During the First World War, my father was aboard the S.S. *Persia* when she was torpedoed in the Med. For three days he was in an open boat and for a long time the family didn't know if he was alive or dead. Then one day the then vicar of Beaulieu, the Reverend Robert Powles, came to see my father's first wife to tell her that he was sure my father was alive.

"He said he had seen my father quite clearly, walking down the village street in front of him. 'If he were dead,' he said, 'he would have been walking behind me.'

"Immediately afterwards the news came that my father was safe."

Mr. Powles was the last of the "independent" vicars of Beaulieu before it came under diocesan control in 1939. Until then it had been one of its jealously guarded rights, granted at the Dissolution, that its parish owed no allegiance to the bishop—the incumbent being the Lord of the Manor's private chaplain as well as Parish priest.

"Mr. Powles enjoyed this freedom to the full," said Lord Montagu. "He was a terrific character. He called himself the Abbot of Beaulieu and would dress himself in abbot's clothes—mitre and all."

Mr. Powles was not only convinced that the monks of Beaulieu existed, he claimed he had struck up an acquaintance with them, and referred to them by name.

"People got to asking him how they were," said Lord Montagu, "and he would reply: 'Oh, Brother Norman was sick today' or something like that. He even held special services in the closed church just for them, usually on Christmas Eve."

Colonel Cadogan, who was then Beaulieu Administrator, told us that during the First World War, his mother used to attend the parish church in the grounds. One Sunday she remarked on the small size of the congregation to Mr. Powles, and he told her: "It's bigger than you can see."

Lord Montagu has been told by people who were stationed on the Manor during the last war that more than one officer was brought up short by the sight of a brown-clad monk wandering around within the closely-guarded confines.

Another person who shared Mr. Powles' belief in the

ghost-monks of Beaulieu was Miss Aimée Cheshire, who lived in a flat in the Domus for many years. There she frequently heard the monks at their devotions, and anyone who had experienced a supernatural event would go and discuss it with her.

Not long after Miss Cheshire died, the elderly nurse companion of another member of the staff, a Mrs. Samuels, was standing on the veranda outside her flat, overlooking the ruined cloisters of the old Abbey, when she saw a monk standing framed in the fifth arch along. She was able to watch him for several minutes before he disappeared and later described him minutely and accurately and said he had been holding a scroll.

Our first port of call at Beaulieu after being filled in on the background by Lord Montagu and Colonel Cadogan was to the home of Colonel and Mrs. Robert Gore-Browne who lived in an isolated house beyond the wine press and replanted the flourishing vineyards which have lain fallow since the monks left Beaulieu. Lord Montagu intends eventually to serve this homegrown wine in the restaurant.

Colonel Gore-Browne saw his ghost like this: "I was taking the dog out for a walk round about dusk, following the lane that goes past this house. Some way ahead and walking towards me I saw a figure in brown, with a skirt that reached to the ground.

"I thought it was a woman, actually. I only had to go down a small dip and up again before we passed each other. But when I got to the brow of the little hill there wasn't anybody there. I looked on either side of the path and I'm pretty sure she wasn't there, either. It may have been a ghost, it may not. I'm suspending my judgement. The dog didn't make a fuss. But some funny things do go on around here, that I do know.

"When we first came to the house we had a Swiss parlourmaid, who definitely saw a ghost. She had come back late from a party—she didn't drink, incidentally—and gone up to her room, switching on the light in the passage to see her way. When she opened the door the light from the passage flooded in and showed her that there was a man lying on the sofa in her room. By the time she had run away and fetched us he had disappeared, but she was able to describe him perfectly: a bright red face with white whiskers.

"Well, we didn't think any more about it until, some time later, a friend of mine told me his uncle had lived here.

"I said, 'Don't tell me he had a bright red face and white whiskers' and my friend looked at me amazed and replied, 'How did you know?' "

Our next call was to the home of Mr. Michael Sedgwick and his mother, whose cottage stood with a few others at the back and slightly to the east of the ruins of the Abbey church. Mr. Sedgwick, who has a great and knowledgeable love of cars, is Research Director for the Motor Museum. It was from him we heard the first personal account of the chanting.

"The first time I heard it was just before Christmas 1959," he said. "I had a lot of work to do and had been up typing and chain-smoking until the early hours. I decided to open the windows and air the room a bit before I went to bed.

"When I opened the window I heard it quite distinctly: it was definitely chanting, and very beautiful chanting. It came in uneven waves, as if from a faulty wireless—sometimes quite loud and then fading away. It was just as if a Catholic mass was being played on the radio in the next flat, but I thought it was curious that someone should have the radio on at that time of night. Anyway, it was so

174

beautiful that I tried to find it on my own wireless. I tell you, I went through every blessed programme there was—French, Italian, everything—and I couldn't find it.

"Later I was told it was just a common or garden supernatural phenomenon. And as a matter of fact it had occurred on the night that someone in the village had died.

"The second time I heard it was also when I was up late working, and also on the eve of a burial. I didn't bother to try and pick it up on the wireless that time."

Mr. Sedgwick's account was later confirmed for us by Mrs. Bertha Day, Beaulieu's catering manageress, who heard it as she returned home late one night up the driveway, the same night before Christmas.

"Suddenly I heard this singing," she told us, "just like a service being held in the church. I knew that Mrs. Mears, a local lady, had died. The following day I asked the vicar if he had held any kind of requiem service for her—just to make sure. He said he hadn't. It was lovely singing, I'll always remember it—it gave you a wonderful feeling of peace."

There is a tradition at Beaulieu that the Sedgwick cottage is haunted. Joan Grant, the psychically-gifted author of *Winged Pharaoh*, lived there for a time and maintained that it had more than one ghost.

Mr. Sedgwick and his mother thought so, too. There are footsteps which pad along the corridor at night. On the whole they were'nt worried about it. But there was a night towards the end of 1960 which was not so easy to overlook.

"Our sitting-room window overlooked a piece of land which is believed to be the monks' burial ground," said Mr. Sedgwick. "It's on the north east side of the church where, traditionally, the monks always put their dead.

"We were sitting there one night when, through the

175

window, came the sounds of feet walking slowly and heavily as if men were carrying a burden. You could hear every bit of their progress, even the different sound their footsteps made when they crossed the bridge over the stream. When we looked out we couldn't see a thing, but the sounds came very close until there were thumps and thuds as if someone were digging in the garden.

"Since, I believe, monks usually carried out their funerals at night, it seems likely we were hearing the re-enactment of a burial."

No trace has ever been found of the dead monks of Beaulieu. But, as Lord Montagu pointed out, the monks kept true to their vow of poverty in this respect, and were buried only in their shrouds, so this lack of evidence isn't surprising.

Mr. Sedgwick was the first person to indicate to us that the Palace house itself might be haunted. Until then all the evidence we had been given told only of ghosts in the grounds or near the Abbey church.

"It isn't anything you can pin down," he said, "but I don't like to be in Palace House in the early hours of the morning. The times when it has been necessary for me to work there alone in my office late at night have been distinctly uncomfortable.

"I don't care to be watched—and that's the feeling I get."

Curiously enough, at the very next house we visited, Tom and I found someone who shared this trepidation.

The Hon. Mrs. Varley, Lord Montagu's half-sister, spent her childhood at Palace House and suffered quite considerable fear at times. She now lives in a cottage in the village, near the Mill.

She said, "My mother was Scottish and terribly in-terested in the supernatural. Whether or not I inherited anything from her, I don't know. But I do know thet I was very frightened as a child in that house. When I was very young I went into the lower drawing-room which is now the large dining-room and came out having been terrified by what I described as 'someone in a lot of smoke'— although the room was empty."

More recently that sense of fear was brought back to her. Mrs. Varley, who once ran a film company which made commercials and documentaries, had brought down a film unit to take night shots on location at Palace House for a film they were making.

"I was in charge of the production side and I had hired quite the best and toughest bunch of electricians in the country to do the lighting. We were to film all night, so we waited until everyone had gone home, locked ourselves in and began shooting. We had power cables leading from the lower to the upper floors.

"Halfway through the night, one of the electricians went downstairs to attend to something, and when he came back he was obviously very frightened. He asked me if there was a nightwatchman on duty in the house. When I said 'No', he looked more scared than ever. I never quite found out what had happened to frighten him so. Whatever it was, it was enough for all those skilled, tough electricians to refuse point blank to go downstairs unaccompanied again.

"Later on that night one of my assistants went downstairs on an errand. As he was going down the staircase, he heard footsteps coming down behind him. He thought it was one of us, coming to chase him up and he said over his shoulder, 'It's all right. I'm going.'

"He told me he was never so frightened in his life as when the footsteps came on *and passed him*, although he saw nobody."

"Did you feel anything?" I asked Mrs. Varley.

"I did a bit. I must admit I wasn't happy, and there was a strong smell of incense about."

Mrs. Varley has also heard the chanting, although it was some years ago. It was impressive to hear her use the same analogy—a spasmodically fading wireless—that Mr. Sedgwick had.

"It was a hot summer's night, very late, and I was sitting on my window seat looking out with my Pekingese beside me. I was about eighteen at the time and I expect I was thinking about some young man I fancied myself in love with—I know I wasn't thinking about the monks or ghosts, or anything like that.

"I was so deep in my thoughts that it had been going on for quite a while before I became conscious of it. What first made me aware of it was the frissons of cold that started to run up and down my back. It was the sound of many voices in repetitive singing, which faded and strengthened like the sound from a primitive wireless. At first I thought it was a wireless in the servants' hall.

"But the sound wasn't coming from there. I couldn't tell you where it *was* coming from. Then the dog began to howl and I got really frightened. I jumped into bed and pulled the sheets right over me. The Peke hid under the eiderdown.

"The next morning I told everybody what I had heard and they tried to laugh me out of it and said I'd probably heard gipsies singing. But an archaeologist friend who was staying with us said that as far as he knew there weren't any gipsies in the neighbourhood, and asked me to sing the tune to him. It was pretty well carved into my memory, so I sang it. He told me it was a well-known Gregorian chant.

"The whole thing preyed on my mind, and when they

178

said to me, 'If you think you've heard something super-natural, why not go and talk it over with Miss Cheshire,' I decided I would. Miss Cheshire was very psychic.

"When I got to her house I didn't know how to broach the subject. She got the tea and I strummed on the piano in her sitting-room. Almost without thinking, I picked out the tune of the chant, and Miss Cheshire turned to me and said, 'So you heard it too. It was so loud last night, that I thought someone else besides myself would hear it.'

"After that I didn't hear it again for a long time. But when I came here to this cottage I did. In fact, about three or four years ago it seemed as if you could hardly put your head out of the window at night without hearing the chanting. It's slackened off lately, though."

I ought to mention here that at the Sedgwick cottage Tom Corbett had discovered traces of what he said were "a very unhappy man and woman who died here once—I think by their own hand."

Mrs. Varley, whose knowledge of the history of the cottage goes back a long way, told us that he was exactly right and that there had been a double tragedy concerning a young husband and wife, resulting in both their deaths at the cottage.

Mrs. Varley sipped her drink thoughtfully. "I don't know what to think about the things that happen at Beaulieu," she said. "Obviously something supernatural is going on. Of course, Marconi may be right. I always liked his theory that no sound is lost, it just travels out into the ether and that, if only science could find a way to recapture it, we might one day be able to hear Christ giving the Sermon on the Mount. Perhaps some freak of nature has brought back again the chanting that was heard at Beaulieu hundreds of years ago. I just don't know."

It is a theory that Tom Corbett and I had heard before,

and one which Tom has never subscribed to, and I eventually rejected.

Even if it explained away the chanting—and I don't think it does—it just won't cover the frequent appearances of the monks. That they are some sort of televisual mirage that freak radio waves have flashed on to the Beaulieu screen is placing too much of a burden on natural laws. You can bend over backwards to try and find scientific explanations for their appearance, and end up in the realms of fantasy.

The simplest, and therefore most logical explanation, to my mind at any rate, is that they are plain ghosts.

Tom said of the monks: "I believe that they are haunting Beaulieu because they don't know where else to go." And I think he has found the heart of the matter.

Whether the ghosts that have been seen so often at Beaulieu are really just one man being seen in many different places or not, we don't know. Tom's own view was that there was more than one, and certainly the people who have heard the chanting refer to it as having the power of "many voices". There is one point that is clear: the ghost is that of a lay brother.

Now the lay brothers of the monasteries were simple men, most of them illiterate, who gave themselves body and soul into monastic keeping. They disappeared from the scenes about 1340, the time of the Black Death. But until that date they were very much in evidence.

Whatever rigours of manual labour they had to undergo, they were, at least, never called on to think for themselves. The monastery did their thinking for them, it fed them, it told them how to order their lives right down to the tiniest detail. My own theory is that when they were set free of this friendly tyranny by death, they were lost.

If you grant that there is a life after death, then the

position of the lay brother when they died resembles very closely that of the monastery servants at the Dissolution, who found themselves thrown out into a strange, secular world where they were no longer protected and secure. But at least the various servants at the Abbey had had some connection with the great outside. The lay brothers had none. They were barred from taking holy orders, and in the Cistercian order they knew nothing of the mind-broadening resources of reading and writing and thinking for themselves.

It is not illogical to suppose that death found some of them completely unprepared to face the initial isolation and decision that seem to lie beyond it, and, like children, they bound themselves frantically to the one spot on earth that they knew and where they had been safe.

This is, of course, complete theory on my part, following up Tom's tentative, but exceedingly likely belief that "they don't know where else to go".

Much of it depends on what you believe to be the mechanics of ghosthood, how it comes about and why. I shouldn't be human if, after all I have seen and heard during the visits we have made to the haunted houses of England, I hadn't formed conclusions of my own. For what they are worth, I proffer them, along with Tom Corbett's findings, in the next and last chapter.

Conclusions

❋ ❋

THERE IS, sadly enough for a journalist like myself, no easy generalisation to be made about ghosts. At each house we visited I thought, "Aha, so *this* is what makes ghosts tick." But always, at the very next house, I would discover some new facet of haunting that completely threw out my theory.

At first I thought that a ghost was a certain type of person who has died, but who, through some defect in character, has stayed on to haunt. But the definition isn't that simple. As I have tried to show, there are mad ghosts and wise ghosts, bad ghosts, kindly ghosts, protective ghosts, silly ghosts—as many types of ghosts, in fact, as there are sides to human nature.

What is it, then, that makes some people haunt and others not? Obviously, not everybody who dies becomes a ghost, otherwise those who are psychic would be aware of shouldering through deep crowds of assorted shades every time they moved.

Therefore, there is some thread of a common denominator that binds those who do become ghosts tightly to the earth, but which others escape. To find it we will have to begin at the beginning.

I hope that by now there will be no doubt in anybody's mind that a far greater proportion of people in this country are psychic than has hitherto been realised by the public. Nearly half the people we encountered in the stately homes had this attribute to a greater or lesser degree. By this I mean that nearly half of them had experienced some supernatural event. If they had not been psychic they could not have had such an experience. Only if you are tuned in to the fourth dimensional wavelength, however weakly, can you be laid open to the sounds and visions that emit from it. If you are not psychic ghosts can be fluttering thick as autumn leaves around you, and you will be completely unaware of them. If you are, the sense can lie dormant for years until you cross the path of a ghost.

Why this extra-sensory gift is given to some people and not to others is as difficult to explain as to say why Mozart was composing fine music at the age of nine.

Tom Corbett has this psychic perception to the point of genius level and in him it is a multi-branched gift. Not only does he act as a sensitive radio receiver for the sounds and images of ghosts, but in many cases he has foresight as well. In his consulting room at his London house in Sloane Gardens he receives a steady stream of eminent business and professional men and women who have learned to rely on his gift and get his forecast before making any financial or far-reaching personal move. And they are not fools.

I remember once my husband and I telling Tom about a business venture in which a friend of ours was going to invest a considerable amount of money. At the time it seemed the smart thing for our friend to do—the venture was being commended all round as a copper-bottomed certainty of a success. Only Tom turned up his nose and boded no good. He was right, of course. The enterprise crashed.

At other times this second sight of his acts as a sort of mental telepathy. At Burford Priory, when the Mother

Prioress was leading us round that lovely house with the graceful, unhurried stride that seems peculiar to nuns, Tom suddenly turned to her and asked if she wouldn't like to rest for a moment. "You have a pain in your leg, haven't you?" he said. Surprised, the Mother Prioress answered that indeed she had, and inquired how Mr. Corbett had known. "I've got it, too," said Tom, simply.

It is a haphazard thing, this gift of his, but wherever and on whatever it works, it is always deadly accurate. At no time does Tom go into anything like a trance, but if he is going through a house haunted by several ghosts and concentrating hard on finding them, he is usually exhausted by the time he comes away—and very often is completely unable to remember anything he said or did during the visit. The constant dovetailing between Tom's findings and those of the many psychics in the stately homes shows, if I may stress it just once more, that the discoveries of neither were merely fortuitous.

Tom Corbett, then, is an accurate ghost finder—now for the ghosts themselves.

Everyone has their own idea of ghosts. To Shakespeare they were the vengeful, doom-carrying Cassandras of the spirit world. To Rupert Brooke they were the nostalgic shades who danced their sly, nightly dance beneath English trees. But in what, for lack of a better term, I must call real life, they are neither so romantic nor so straightforward. Men and women never are—and ghosts are men and women who have died, that's all.

The man whose picture of the after life in its primary stages most closely approximates to the image that was gradually built up before me, as I followed Tom Corbett around and listened and learned, is St. John Irvine. In his novel, *Sophia*, he presents a most reasonable delineation of the time immediately following death. He assumes, as it is most logical to assume if you believe in a survival, that the soul, sex, character and mind of a person remain intact, and the only thing death takes away from you is your body. *Sophia* begins with the death of a country parson's wife who is surprised to find that she is dead, but still essentially the same person, only lacking flesh and blood. All her teaching and education find her completely unprepared to face the fact that she is in a sort of no-man's land, a limbo of a first halt, where nothing has changed except that she is invisible to her family.

Although she finds that, by exerting her will, she can travel, she is reluctant to leave the security of her home and the people she loves. Aimlessly she wanders around her home and garden. One by one she is joined by other unseen spirits who have also recently died and who are all bewildered at this hiatus in the scheme of things. Gradually they find that there is as much progress to be made in death as there was in life, as much climbing and striving. Sophia realises that she must let the living get on with their lives while she begins her long climb up . . . to what, Mr. Irvine doesn't specify, and it is not my province to guess at—I have stamped on too many denominational toes as it is.

This picture of what immediately follows death fits in exactly as a background to Tom's findings. It seems obvious to anyone who has studied ghosts that there must be some sort of ante-chamber in which they are first received which is not so far removed from life, and from which everybody eventually advances—the length of time they stay in it depends on themselves. So purely on my own initiative, and in no sense being dogmatic about it, I am adopting this combination of ideas from St. John Irvine and Tom Corbett as a basis for my argument.

It seems that in the main ghosts are probably those who

have been unable to adjust themselves to death's conditions, and cling to their old home and surroundings rather than face what lies beyond them, rather as the insecure cling to their childhood instead of facing adult life. This is a rule that exceptions destroy time and time again. But it is a fair guide.

It can be love that binds them, or hate, or even a self-imposed blind ignorance. Those ghosts like the monks at Beaulieu, the old night watchman at Sawston Hall, and the monk at Burford Priory, who haunt habitually and monotonously, carrying out the customs they observed in life, not realising that centuries of wasted time are flying by, seem to lack, not intelligence exactly, but a certain spiritual energy and awareness that is necessary to their advancement. They will go on in time, of course, for they must, but to do so needs a decision and independence of will that can take aeons of time to acquire.

Lady Louisa Carteret, for instance, in her deathly-cold corridor at Longleat, is still wallowing in the misery and general hate that arose out of the injury done to her two centuries ago. One supposes that one day she will wake up to the futility of it, but until then she is whirling in a vortex of her own suffering that would be pathetic if it took a less forbidding form.

Such ghosts as these are constant. I don't mean they are permanent fixtures—they will fade in time. But for the duration they haunt incessantly. They are like direct currents of electricity which psychics automatically plug into every time they cross their path.

Really there ought to be some differentiation between the various types of spirits. To lump them all under the title of "ghosts" is misleading. Take the men and women who, after their death, have felt a desperate need to say "good-bye" to a friend or some near relative and by a supernatural effort are able to fulfil that need and make a brief, final appearance. I have mentioned two such instances in the introductory chapter of this book—the nun who appeared for a few seconds to her favourite pupil and the soldier who gave a farewell salute to Robert Graves a few weeks after his (the soldier's) death—and I know of many more such occurrences. They are not constant ghosts and should not be put in that category. In most cases they are never seen again. They have done their best to show that all is well with them and, presumably, have then passed on to new pastures.

In a different category again are the "warning" ghosts—those which appear to give notice of a forthcoming death or calamity. They are as different from those unfortunate, unhappy earth-bound spectres as chalk from cheese. Presumably, they have managed to see the disaster and returned, briefly, to warn against it. Whether they think they are doing any good or not is beyond me. The disaster always happens anyway. The dog that Robert Graves mentioned at his in-laws' home in Wales, the little sailor boy that appeared to the Sheridan family and the appearance of Nell Gwynne to George Cornwallis-West at Salisbury Hall were all giving notice of tragedies that nobody was able to avert.

If they had been able to speak, now, it might have been a different matter. But ghosts are rarely vocal. Tom Corbett tells me that it takes vast effort and ectoplasmic energy to appear at all, let alone talk. The reason, he says, that ghosts so often appear as indistinct, grey, shadowy figures is because they have not been able to summon up the strength to complete their colour transformation. The Colonel's dog, created by Thorne Smith in his Topper books, which could not manage to materialise beyond his tail and rump, is, perhaps, not so far from the truth. Tom

Corbett once saw a pair of shoes with feet up to the ankle in them, walking along a farm track. His sixth sense was able to pick up the image of the woman whose feet they were, but her effort at materialisation had been a grotesque failure.

Another category of ghosts that really require different nomenclature are the guides, who do not haunt in the strict sense of the word, but hover around the earth in a deliberate attempt to help lost and bewildered souls to help themselves. I really can't explain them because I don't know enough about them. But there seems no doubt that they are there, and, if Clare Sheridan is to be believed, Father John, the priest that Tom Corbett found in the chapel at Brede, is one of them and his mission is to set free the embodied souls that have shackled themselves to earth.

Then, again, there are the "approving" ghosts. A few of these fall into the first category, having bound themselves to a spot on earth that they adored in life and refuse to leave in death. The Thynne who built Longleat is an example of this type, a constant ghost who blindly insists on spending eternity in the surroundings he knows. But most of these ghosts are transitory—only occasionally returning to earth to manifest their approval to their descendants or successors over what they are doing for the old home. Mr. Frewen's grandmother at Brede and Sir John Dashwood's mother at West Wycombe Park seem to be typical examples of this earth-pulling love.

Perhaps a scientific investigation into ghosts would discover other categories and other reasons for haunting. But, on the whole, I think these are the main ones.

Just as there is no limit to the type of ghosts, there seems to be no limit to their style of haunting. Some ghosts seem unaware that time has passed and conditions have changed since they were alive, while others are fairly modern in their outlook.

There are ghosts, for instance, who stubbornly walk on floor levels that no longer exist, or play on spinets that have been firewood for centuries, or ring bells that were melted down long ago. Whether they are echoes from the past, whether they are blind to the fact that things have changed, or whether old habits die hard, it is difficult to say.

The cavalier at Salisbury Hall is the perfect example of an old-fashioned ghost. He walks a floor that disappeared in the 1800s and appears through a doorway that is now bricked up. On the other hand, the monks at Beaulieu seem aware of prevailing conditions since they sing requiem mass every time someone on the estate, or in the village, dies. In fact, the time system seems to vary for each ghost.

It should not be thought that only the past produces ghosts. It is true that most of the spirits which Tom Corbett discovered came from a time not later than the Industrial Revolution, but there are later ghosts —the grandmother at Brede, for instance. And I often wonder whether a ghost in modern dress would be recognised as such. We have got used to the idea that ghosts come from the romantic ages. And, quite frequently, unless a ghost is sending out chilling rays of cold they are only recognised as phantoms because of their old-fashioned dress.

After all, if you woke up at night to see a figure in flannels and sports jacket walk across your bedroom floor, you would assume that he was a burglar quicker than you would think 'It's a ghost'. And if the figure had disappeared before you could get to it, you would believe that he had made a clever getaway before you got your wits about you, rather than believe that he had, literally, gone into thin air. Whereas if a lady in a ruff walked across the bedroom floor you would, discounting practical jokers, come to the conclusion immediately that she was a ghost, not a burglar.

Fear of ghosts is largely convention. Many a person has seen a spectre without the slightest hastening of their heart-beats. The shock has come later, when the realisation that it was a supernatural body sank in, but this shock has been largely conditioned in us by the fictional view of ghosts as blood-curdling, throat-cutting monsters—a picturesque image with no connection with reality.

In actual fact, ghosts are not harmful, by which I mean that they cannot pick up a knife and stab you, or freeze you to death with horror. They are capable of influence, as Tom Corbett warned the Duke of Bedford. But the harm that comes from inhabiting a badly haunted house or wing is the same as the harm that comes from bad companions—if you are easily influenced, then you will be influenced for the worse.

There is no doubt that exorcism by the Church is an extremely efficient method of getting rid of ghosts. But Tom Corbett is against it: "It is all very well sending them away," he says, "but where are you sending them to?" His argument is that the chronic and constant ghosts should be helped—not merely sent away into an outer darkness. He believes that humans should establish some sort of contact with the ghosts that haunt their houses, should talk to them and try to make them realise the futility of what they are doing.

There is more than one house in Britain that has managed to get rid of its ghosts by this method. Perhaps the owners do not actually talk to the ghosts, but they accept them and tolerate them, thus establishing a warm, human link that, in time, is just as effective.

Littlecote is a perfect example. There is no doubt that at

one time this house was quite badly haunted by a very unsettled phantom indeed. The Wills family made no attempt to exorcise it, they just went on living their contented lives, accepting the ghost as a fairly normal phenomenon. The ghost has not been seen or felt for many years now, and, according to Tom, has faded happily away, escaping the prison of its own grief.

Another good example is the case of Martha, who haunted the dell at Brede. Clare Sheridan said that she established contact with Martha and talked to her. Until then Martha had been a typical, chronic ghost, stuck in a limbo of guilt and ignorance. Under the influence of her friendship with Mrs. Sheridan she was making progress and beginning to realise that she must advance. Now she has been exorcised. Tom Corbett only hopes that the exorcism did not come too soon and that she wasn't banished to a place where she would be even more restless.

I realise that there are tremendous gaps in this attempt of mine to explain what ghosts are. It is, of course, complete theory. My only justification for making it at all is that it is what I most firmly believe.

There are, however, two statements that I can make in the complete assurance that they are truths. The first is that trenchant sceptics who say there is no life after death because "no one has ever come back to prove it", are batting on an extremely sticky wicket. The second is that if ghosts were deductible, the great majority of the stately homes of England would be considerably better off than they are at the moment.